THE *Butterfly Customer*

Capturing the Loyalty of Today's Elusive Consumer

SUSAN M. O'DELL • JOAN A. PAJUNEN

John Wiley & Sons Canada, Ltd

Toronto • New York • Chichester • Weinheim • Brisbane • Singapore

John Wiley & Sons Canada, Ltd
22 Worcester Road
Etobicoke, Ontario
M9W 1L1

Canadian Cataloguing in Publication Data

O'Dell, Susan M.
  The butterfly customer : capturing the loyalty of today's elusive consumer

Rev.ed.
Includes bibliographical references and index.
ISBN 0-471-64518-4

1.Customer services. 2.Customer relations. 3.Relationship marketing.
I. Pajunen, Joan. II. Title.

HF5415.5.033 2000   658.8'12   *C00-93142-5*

Production Credits
Cover & text design: JAQ
Cover photograph: The Image Bank
Printer: Tri-Graphic Printing Limited
Copy Editor: Ron Edwards

Printed in Canada
10 9 8 7 6 5 4 3 2 1

DEDICATION

To partners, personal and professional, without whom nothing could remain in harmony.

C O N T E N T S

An Update from the Authors   ix
Preface   xiv
Acknowledgements   xxii

Chapter One: Butterfly Behaviour   1
This Trend Could Have Been Predicted   2
The Eight Characteristics of the Butterfly Customer   3
A New Breed of Customer   10
The Search for Elusive Customer Loyalty   11
Where is Business Today?   13
Butterfly Nets   14
Can the Butterfly Customer Ever Be Loyal?   18

Chapter Two: Breaking Trust With the Customer   19
The Trust Factor   19
Who Do You Trust?   21
Are Trust Levels Declining?   22
In Business We Trust   24
The Uh-oh Feeling   25
A String of Broken Promises   27
The High Cost of Low Trust   30
The Rewards of Trust   33

Chapter Three: The Return of the Monarch   **35**
The Five Characteristics of the Monarch   35
Can You Earn the Customers Trust?   40
How Does the Business Build Trust With the Butterfly?   44
Be Credible in All Aspects   46

Chapter Four: The Service Kaleidoscope   **49**
The Three Dimensions of the Business Kaleidoscope   50
Three Dimensions Create Endless Variety   53
Harmony in 3-D—The Key to Building Trust   56
The Cause of Disharmony   60
Promise What You Deliver   62
A New Measure of Business Success   66

Chapter Five: Measuring the Trust Account   **67**
What Is the Trust Account?   67
Protecting the Trust Account Balance   70
The Opening Balance Sets the Tone   70
How Does A Company Measure Its Trust Account?   72
Learn To "See Your Business Feelingly"   73
The 3-D Audit   77

Chapter Six: Conducting a 3-D Audit   **81**
The 3-D Audit Objective   82
Step One: Engage the Team   83
Step Two: Feast On the Facts   87
Step Three: Feel the Experience   90
Step Four: Gauge the Gaps   94
Step Five: Describe the Harmony   95
Step Six: Engage the Team...Again   97
Berean Then and Now   98
From the Specific to the General   100

Chapter Seven: No Strategy   **103**
What is Strategy?   104
What is Your Strategy?   104

The Four F Behaviour 106
Focus: Create Common Ground 106
Faithful: Keep the Goal In Sight 111
Flexible: Use a Pencil Not a Pen 115
Fast: A Quick Turnaround 117
Involve the Team 119
Focused, Faithful, Flexible, Fast 120

Chapter Eight: The Expectations Contract: Misreading the Customer 121
Hidden Expectations 121
Competitive Chaos 123
The Economic Atmosphere 128
The Consumer Moods 131
What is My Customer Feeling Today? 135

Chapter Nine: The Media: Attractive Offer or Fatal Attraction? 141
Glasses for the Masses 142
A Campaign Which Supports Corporate Strategy 145
No Gap Between the Media Tactics and the
   Campaign Goal 147
An Involved and Committed Team 150
A 3-D Match 153
Guarding Against Creating a Fatal Attraction 155

Chapter Ten: The Physical Dimension: The Emperor's New Clothes 159
Test the Associations 161
Live in the Customer's Shoes 168
Pass the Real World Test 176
Closing the Gap in the Physical Dimension 178

Chapter Eleven: The People Dimension: No Value Added 181
Lessons From the Price Wars 182
Are Your Employees Adding Value? 183
Select the Right Service Strategy 184
Are Your People *Able* to Add Value? 195
Mystery Customers 202

Chapter Twelve: Internal Affairs: Culture Clash   205

What is Corporate Culture?   205
A 3-D Decision Process   207
Complete Communications   211
3-D Leadership   215
A 3-D Company   218

Chapter Thirteen: The Service-Empowered Team   219

What Are Empowered People?   220
What Are Service-Empowered People?   222
Everyone Has a 3-D Job Description   224
People Are Selected Because They Will Thrive   226
Education: Beyond Training and Development   229
Rewards and Consequences   234
It is Time to Let Go   236

Chapter Fourteen: Exercises in 3-D   239

Exercise #1 Seeing Things Feelingly: The Subconscious
  Recorder   242
Exercise #2 Trust: Monarch or Butterfly?   243
Exercise #3 Strategy: The Crystal Ball   245
Exercise #4 The Service Kaleidoscope: Snapshots
  in 3-D   246
Exercise #5 A 3-D Company: Empowered or Entrapped? 247
Adapt, Borrow, Integrate, Reject   249

Conclusion   251
A 3-D Reading List   255
Index   261

AN UPDATE FROM THE AUTHORS

We only wish we had had to re-write this book in order to re-release it.

It would be delightful to report that more businesses had discovered the simple strategy that turns The Butterfly Customer—a creature constantly in motion, seeking the best deal, the greatest choice, the latest trend—into a loyal Monarch. We hoped we could relay the news that customers themselves would now report a greater degree of loyalty to the retail and service sector.

But alas, in preparation for the paperback release, when we asked our research partners to once again listen to the inner voice of the consumer, we heard the same old theme—there is too big a gap between what is being promised and what is being delivered. The result of that gap? Customers who continue to be delighted by the plethora of new offers, while still pining for an era when promises were not given lightly, and broken rarely.

PLUS ÇA CHANGE

On the surface, the world of the consumer has changed greatly from when we first wrote the book. Internet commerce has accelerated beyond predicted expectations. Martha Stewart heads a billion-dollar lifestyle business that has consumers happily incorporating "Good Things" into every room in their home. Former titans Eaton's in Canada have disappeared, while upstarts like Just for Feet in the U.S. have come and gone with nary a trace. Traditional retailers like Barnes and Noble struggle in the on-line battle against nimble players like Amazon.com.

So while consumers face a very different landscape than they did a couple of years ago—at least when it comes to the names on the marquee or the locations of the store—when it comes to loyalty, the more things have changed, the more they have stayed the same.

One key message of the book confirmed by our recent research is that traditional interpretations of loyalty are out-dated. Customers consider themselves loyal to a company (from 39% to 73% depending on the sector), but do not equate that loy-alty with exclusivity. What they do offer their preferred retail and service providers is top-of-mind awareness, frequent visits, and the gift of referrals. But even this magnitude of attachment to a company isn't the ultimate loyalty goal.

LOYAL ISN'T AS LOYAL DOES; LOYAL IS AS LOYAL FEELS

When we probed the nuances of what customers feel in our recent research, we continued to find that the loyalty thread is tenuous. For instance, when asked what motivates customers to abandon a "loyal" relationship with a service provider, the issue of return policies scored unbelievably high. In the customer's view, "satisfaction guaranteed" means more than "take the goods back." It also means "take responsibility for selling defective goods in the first place" and "be honest about what you will do for me."

Listen to these comments from customers who had left a long-term relationship with a service provider and ask yourself if this could be your customer talking:

> *"They refused to take back a defective hose with a rip near the end, told me to just cut it shorter. I ripped up my (loyalty) card right there."*

> *"When I bought it, they promised it was refundable, but when I returned it they refused to take it back."*

> *"Promised a refund at time of purchase, but only offered a credit when I came back."*

We didn' t plant the words "promised me" into customers' vocabulary in the survey. They popped up from the subconscious place where customers record all your messages and keep an on-going report card of how well you do in delivering what you say you will.

And given the dismal state of service sector scores on our research report card, it is no wonder that consumers continue to approach retail and service companies in a state of mistrust. They enter the door skeptical that you ever intended to deliver what you promised, much less that you are able to do so.

> *"Promised me I had their 'preferred customer' rate, but several other companies phoned and offered me lower rates. When I called to transfer my service, I was then offered the same rate as the competition [had offered me]. Why didn't they make me this offer in the first place?"*

> *"They made a billion-dollar profit and yet raised my service fees."*

The greatest loyalty factor is how closely customers perceive what you have promised them, compared to what in fact is delivered. Whether it is product quality, service, low prices, or return practices, customers report that all too often there is a gap between what is said and what is done.

The secret to true customer loyalty is to build trust. And to build trust you must:

1. Understand the implicit and explicit promises your customers receive from you and about you.
2. Consistently deliver those promises in all the details, in every dimension of the business.

TRUST IS A VIRTUAL COMMODITY

Trust is not just valuable in the traditional retail or service model where ads are created to lure consumers into stores filled with merchandised product and ready-to-serve staff. In fact, trust as a business success factor is even more compelling in the on-line world where The Butterfly can not only prove elusive, but can be invisible.

Is Amazon.com a real company with whom customers can form a relationship or is it just another distribution channel that could just as easily be an 800 # with pictures? How susceptible will it be as brand names enter the fray? Imagine, Oprahbooks.com, or Book-of-the-Month-Club.com. How loyal are its customers compared to those of Marthastewart.com where customers actually feel they have a relationship with the business as measured by energetic chat rooms, and the personality of the business is woven through every page, every order form, every contact? It is possible to make impersonal cyberspace very personal indeed, but it is not accomplished by building an extensive e-mailing list with which to bombard customers with additional offers.

In fact, understanding the ambiguous role of traditional mailing lists and reward programs in retaining loyalty is critical in an era when those programs become evermore expensive and complex. The customers we surveyed rated reward programs number 21 on a list of 22 factors that are important for loyalty and we continue to wonder at the magnitude of dollars devoted to chasing the elusive butterfly with something they value so little. Those who re-define loyalty the way their customers do will avoid the entrapment of golden handcuffs—those reward programs that require too high a percentage of the customer's exclusivity or energy.

What is required in every venue where an ongoing relationship with the consumer is critical to growth and profits is a high degree of trust: you promise me only what you can deliver.

So you've told me the story. Why should I bother reading the book?

Because, in the words of one jewellery chain president, "Never again will I be able to visit my stores without hearing that inner voice of the customer nagging me, 'So is what I see really what you promised me?'" He and his team have used *The Butterfly Customer* to create a store visit program that makes sure every ad campaign is matched by the store appearance and staff product knowledge.

Reading this book will cause you to look at your business differently—more like a customer does. But raising your consciousness is not enough. Just like the president cited above, true loyalty requires a series of steps to pay off where the customers feel it most—in the details of their experience with you.

Those who report the greatest value from investing in the book tell us they did three things.

1. First, they kept on their customer hat as they read it, allowing themselves to feel as angry, disappointed or disillusioned as the consumers we quote in the book.

2. Second, they shared it with those in charge of other dimensions of the customer experience. For example, their advertising folks discussed the implications with store designers, and thought through the details with those in charge of operations.

3. Third, they changed the way they made decisions, working hard to get at what it feels like to be a customer, or a staff person serving a customer, before the ad campaign ran, the web page was posted or the return policy decided.

Magic? No. Simple? Yes. What customers want? Absolutely.

And what is the reward for those who have read the book and followed the steps? Customers who not only report loyalty but also feel loyal—that state of mind where the instant gratification of a lower price, or newer offer is not as compelling as what they already have. They have trust in a company that knows that a promise delivered is the only promise worth having.

Consumer Loyalty Index© Consumers of retail, banking and telecommunications surveyed in 1,000 mall intercepts nationwide. The research asked about loyalty perceptions and behaviours. A summary of the work, conducted by **Acumen Research Group** and released April 2000, is available at their Web site www.acumenresearch.com.

To provide comments on the book or for further information about 3-D Audits© or future research, you may contact the co-author, Joan A. Pajunen via e-mail at pajunen@netcom.ca or at **TrendSeek Intl. (416) 410-2449.**

PREFACE

COUNT ME IN...OR COUNT ME OUT?

I want to be the airline traveller whose ticket agent ran across the terminal to pick up his tickets from another airline.

I don't want to be customer number four in the line watching while the ticket agent runs off.

I want to stay in the hotel where the doorman jumped in a plane to deliver a briefcase left behind by a guest.

I don't want to be the shareholder paying the bills.

I want to shop in a store that advertises "Our employees will jump through hoops for you."

I don't like being the employee who never knows what's going to be expected of me next.

No wonder the world of service has never been more schizophrenic or confused. "Count me in!" say those customers who have actually experienced one of those earth-shattering "service moments." But just for a minute, shut out the hype and listen to the other still, small voices within.

> *Don't you have a fleeting moment of compassion for all the other customers who remain in the service shadows while one is basking in the spotlight of single-minded attention?*

> *Doesn't the accountant part of your heart beat a bit faster as you find yourself calculating the cost of these superhuman efforts?*

> *As manager of minimum-wage staff who have to deliver ever-increasing expectations, don't you find yourself struggling, under payroll cuts, just to get the basics done?*

"Hey, count me out!" is what the rest of us would like to shout. And yet, the stories of wondrous, magical service moments have become the currency of the retail and service industries. Their power to excite, enrich, and change forever the way business is done is the stuff of legends.

Thousands of words have been written and millions of dollars have been devoted to achieving loyal customers through delivering incredible service. We have watched organizations:

> *Zap the customer!*

> *Wow the customer!*

> *Customer for life! The customer.*

> *And create quality circles everywhere.*

Frankly, "quality circles" just make us dizzy and the real winners have been the consultants and trainers. What's your bill so far for what has proven to be a most elusive goal?

Like many of our clients, you might well be one of those companies that has spent a million dollars, or one of those managers who has leapt through service hoops trying to create "Raving Fans"[1] only to end up with "Craving Fans."

These are the customer-service junkies who are looking for the highest high and the biggest rush possible from ever-more-incredible feats of service. And then there are the ones who tell great stories about you and drive the expectations of your other customers to unattainable levels.

Customers, even after a decade of expensive "Knock Your Socks Off Service,"[2] flit off to try the newest airline, restaurant, clothing store, bank, or grocer despite imaginative, exciting, and expensive reward programs.

THE BUTTERFLY CUSTOMER

Have you too ended up with a customer base full of high-maintenance clients, who, because of their demands for spectacular and expensive service, lower your profit and still, despite all your costly efforts, vanish to the competition without warning or the slightest hint of remorse?

Welcome to the era of the Butterfly Customer for whom loyalty appears to be a lost virtue—regardless of the time, expense, and effort expended by a business to capture it.

Butterflies flit from service to service, from store to store, from business to business, and from relationship to relationship.

[1] Kenneth Blanchard and Sheldon Bowles, *Raving Fans: A Revolutionary Approach to Customer Service* (New York: Morrow, 1993), p. 7.

[2] Ronald Zemke and Chip R. Bell, *Managing Knock Your Socks Off Service* (New York: AMACOM, 1992).

The newest restaurant sensation bustles with customers, while last week's pet languishes with empty tables. Once unassailable department store icons now struggle through downsizing, bankruptcy protection, or worse. Even brand-name products that once worried only about shifting market share from one to the other, wake up to find no-names the order of the day.

Butterfly Customers are transient visitors to your business who have displaced the loyal customers of the past, despite all your efforts to coax them into staying.

Loyalty and the Butterfly Customer

In the face of this craving, disloyal Butterfly, it is tempting to simply give up on loyalty and switch the dollars and energy into creating ever more exciting concepts or to lures such as a constant emphasis on lower prices. But don't give up on loyalty yet. The bottom line impact of converting the gypsy behaviour of the Butterfly Customer is too great to pass up.

We don't need to read *Harvard Business Review* or listen to service gurus to know the negative effect the flitting Butterfly behaviour has on profits. We need only listen to prospective clients describe their horror stories: twenty years of consistent profits dwindling overnight into a deficit; customer counts fall the moment a new competitor opens; plummeting gross margin dollars and percentages.

The Monarch Customer

Customers have always demonstrated some aspects of Butterfly behaviour. It's just that in the past, that behaviour was more reminiscent of the Monarch than of today's new Butterfly. You know the Monarch. It's the butterfly that flies a predictable course, returning to the same old haunts at the same old time. Year after

year. Loyal as loyal can be. Like the swallows returning to Capis-
trano, the service sector could rely on them and await their return.

Today's Butterfly, however has no such predictability. As we
worked with retail and service companies through the last tumul-
tuous decade, our greatest challenge was to find a way to understand the Butterfly Customer, and to learn what, if anything,
would make them loyal. The best piece of news we found as we
researched the trend is that, in fact, the Butterfly Customer is as
anxious to remain loyal as you are to keep them. But before they
will be loyal, they want, expect, and need something from you.

What does the Butterfly Customer need to become loyal? Just
one thing, to find you worthy of their trust. This is the key to tam-
ing the flitting behaviour of this new Butterfly Customer into a
regular set of patterns. Trust is what will cause the Butterfly Customers of the next millennium to take on the colouring of the
beloved Monarch and once again return to become regular
patrons of your business.

And unlike the demanding and expensive-to-serve Butterfly
Customers spawned by spectacular feats of service, customers
who trust don't expect you to drive your employees crazy or sac-
rifice your operating margins by trying to deliver outrageous or
unrealistic acts of service. Monarch Customers are willing to let
you get on with running your business.

In fact, customers with a high degree of trust take an interest
in the success of your business. In giving you their trust, they
become partners in the experience. They want to make it easy for
your staff to do their job. They accept your right to make a profit. They understand that constant service feats cost you (and ultimately them) more than they are worth.

They allow you to take care of the other key stakeholders in
your business: the staff and the shareholder. Because they are
interested in a lifetime relationship, they want your business and
your staff to be around long enough for everyone to profit.

Customers who trust are willing to return to you, refer others to you, and stick with you, even if it requires some time, money, and effort. These high-profit, low-maintenance customers are your reward for being trustworthy.

These are not customers demonstrating the new Butterfly behaviour, darting about your business, but rather more like the loyal Monarch Customers, following a predictable path as they return time after time, year after year, to do business with you.

EARNING CUSTOMER TRUST

Trust doesn't happen with a single, isolated act of service, no matter how spectacular. It doesn't even happen with outstanding service delivered most of the time. In fact, we find truly trusting customers in some pretty ordinary business environments.

Trust is built by delivering quiet consistency, one transaction at a time. Trust is gained by delivering what you promise, how you promised it, and doing it consistently.

And that is much tougher than it sounds because the customer sees and hears implied promises in every facet of your business. The advertising message you send, the quality of the product, the feel of your environment, and the policies your staff enforce all create an opportunity to build, or break, trust.

The secret of building trust is to deliver what you promise, no more, no less, and to do it with integrity.

WHAT THIS BOOK WILL DO FOR YOU

For the reader who wants to build "elasticity" into customer relationships and is weary of the consultant or service feat of the month, this book offers a straightforward way to look at the business that is not heavily focused on expensive initiatives.

This book takes you on a journey which allows you to

evaluate the level of trust your customers have in you, create a plan to increase that level and then keep it high. It shows you a simple way to measure the emotional trust account in your business and determine how much "latitude" you have earned from your customers.

The book will invite you to see your business as the customer sees it and to feel the experience as they feel it. Here is what you will find in the book.

We first describe the evolution of the Butterfly Customer and reveal how business has created this new consumer by behaving in ways that have broken trust with the customer, frustrating their natural instinct to trust and build relationships with you. And that's the bad news. The good news is that the resulting trust vacuum provides a wonderful opportunity for a business with integrity to awaken the customer's latent desire to trust and create loyal relationships. We then explore how, with three simple dimensions, a business can create a unique experience for the customer and how keeping those three dimensions in harmony is the secret to building trust.

We explain the 3-D Audit process we use to measure the gaps in trust and provide specific recommendations about closing them. And finally, we illustrate how to make every member of your team a steward of your most precious business asset—the trust of all your customers.

This book provides the secret of creating loyalty with the Butterfly Customer in any business from the local Mom and Pop convenience store to the multinational corporation. This secret puts an end, once and for all, to all the expensive, incredible service efforts that have been impossible to sustain.

This book is about creating loyal customers through providing experiences and maintaining an environment in which the customer can trust. Because, by giving your customers a place they can trust, they return the gifts of high profits and low maintenance!

A WORD TO THE BUTTERFLY READER

Whether you are the CEO of a *Fortune 500* company or a fledgling entrepreneur, you also have become one of these Butterfly Customers who visits many and awards loyalty to few. The same is true for you as our reader. We know you are busy, have a desk piled high with "good reading for a quiet day" and that we will have to work hard to earn your trust that our book is worth your time. We also know that you are as curious, suspicious, and intelligent as any of your own customers.

How do we know? The authors combine all the traits of the Butterfly in our partnership, with one of us being the perennial gadfly, constantly on the search for a glimmer of a new idea which can instantly be translated into action, and the other a more cynical analyst who must understand the whys and the wherefores before trusting the value of the idea or insight.

So in this book you will find quick snapshots for those of you who just want to flit through the pages. But, there are also some thought-provoking questions and analysis for those of you who want to delve deeper into the psyche of this new customer with whom we are all trying to do business. Above all, you will find specific ideas about building a relationship with the Butterfly Customer that earns you Monarch Customer loyalty.

We invite you to join with us in exploring the "emotional landscape" of your business. We will dare you to move beyond the comfort zone of facts and figures into the heart and soul of how customers are responding to the ways in which you choose to do business. For it is only through understanding how your customers are feeling that you can finally appreciate how to earn their trust. And it is through earning trust that you earn the rewards coveted by business everywhere—a profitable, successful, easy to maintain business.

ACKNOWLEDGEMENTS

First and foremost this book belongs to clients who have allowed us to show them the service kaleidoscope and the power of 3-D harmony. Whether they let us describe their company in specific detail or asked for more anonymity...without their generosity of spirit, this book could never have been attempted. Judy, Warren, Lorna, Dan, Gene, Patricia, Joey, Donna, Colleen, Dave, Louise...Many thanks.

Service Dimensions Inc. is an association of many independent souls who believe in our unique approach and bring a wide range of skills to our customer needs. They bore the brunt of an extraordinary year during which we doubled our sales and completed this book. Special mention must go to Kim Fulton, Karen Orme, Gary Metcalf, Denise Bilsland, Franca Cambria, Sandy Schell Kennedy, Carla and Susan at the Sussex Centre, and most of all, Susan Allen and Peter Rioux.

While doing research, we encountered many service providers who delivered to us as customers, a 3-D experience of the first order. Here are three. Paul Clarke and Lucia Maresca of the Casa Maresca in Positano gave us a magical week in which to create the book outline. Vincenza, Sonia, and Gino at Toronto's Allo Bistro let us linger (long past closing) over numerous working lunches. Canadian/American Airlines, whose staff exemplify the power of making the impersonal personal whether the flight was an hour or twenty.

We acknowledge those who actually created the book with us.

To Jim Childs, Publisher, Professional and Trade, John Wiley and Sons, Inc., who one summer's day answered his phone and courteously responded to a couple of would-be authors. Jim, you gave us the courage to proceed; let's hope we give you a best-seller.

To Karen Milner, Publisher and Editor, Professional, Reference and Trade, John Wiley and Sons Canada, Ltd, whose clear direction and calm delivery always set us on a path to do better work. Your editorial strength helped us pare down and organize our thoughts into the book we had always intended to write.

To Ron Edwards, who read our fifth draft and practically overnight gave us the inspiration and guidance to turn it into a "10." You will never know how much your opening phrase, "this is really good stuff" meant to two weary writers-in-progress.

To Elizabeth McCurdy, who dealt with two very opinionated authors without ruffling our artistic feathers even once. If you ever tire of this profession, consider hostage negotiation.

And finally, to those who read, re-read, and read again, the fragments that became drafts and finally a finished product. Especially to: Karen Orme, who interviewed clients, drafted stories, checked facts, and believed in this project from the beginning; to Doris O'Dell whose insightful research validated our position on trust and consumer behaviour; to Nadia Bailey whose sense of the dramatic encouraged us to use words, feelingly; and to Bernice Wolman whose tough entrepreneurial eyes kept all three stakeholders in focus. Your insightful comments and straightforward criticisms protected the needs of our audience. We, and they, are grateful.

And on the personal side.

To Ken, Lara, and Wayne. I want to say thanks for the cups of tea delivered at 2:00 am, staying out of my way when I was on the trail of some great, but soon to be edited, turn of phrase, and for taking up the slack in our personal life.

Joan

To Michael, whose endless encouragement brings joy to every dimension in my life.

Susan

CHAPTER ONE

Butterfly Behaviour

On the way home, Mom, or just as likely Dad, rushes to fit in three chores before the long September weekend: hitting the mall for school supplies, the warehouse club for lunchtime snacks, and the discount store for Nike knock-offs.

Meanwhile teens prowl the flea market or second-hand store for clothes "Buy the Pound" and then flock to the trendy part of town for the latest in nose rings or tattoos, Snapple in hand.

The entire family is caught in the rush to outfit budding athletes at the sporting goods super store and still leave time to reach the department store before closing to get T-shirts and socks.

It's the Butterfly Customer. Constantly in motion for the best deal, the greatest choice, the latest trend, this creature selects a store or brand apparently at random, often abandoning the tried and true for the newest, the closest, the cheapest.

It's exhausting to be a Butterfly and disheartening to serve one. There isn't one single store or brand that captures all of their interest, dollars, or oh-so-precious time. Consumers have been transformed from loyal, reliable, and predictable patrons into transients—here today, flitting across the street tomorrow.

THIS TREND COULD HAVE BEEN PREDICTED

In the early decades of this century many customers were loyal because they had no other choice or felt they didn't. Unlike the Butterfly of today, these customers were more like the Monarch, returning to the same locale at the same time, via the same route, year after year.

Your store would have seen them in the spring for gardening supplies, in the fall for back-to-school gear, and again at the holiday season for gifts. Your bank would have opened their first savings account and been certain of getting their first mortgage. Your service would often have been the only game in town, and the Monarchs flocked along their annual route with great predictability.

A generation or two ago, those customers remained loyal because your business, you and your employees, were part of their neighbourhood and to withdraw their support would have been viewed as unneighbourly. These were the decades of brand loyalty, and the ad on the billboard that claimed "I'd walk a mile for a Camel" expressed a very real consumer behaviour—the willingness to pay a personal price for a particular product or service.

Today that billboard would seem dated, not just because it features cigarettes, but because it promotes an emotion most of us can only imagine—consumer willingness to walk a mile for anything.

The last few decades spawned a new customer who has abandoned commitment. Malls with national retail chains pulled shoppers away from downtown local merchants and regional "Davids" fought national "Goliaths" in every industry from transportation to fast food. We saw the emergence of a new breed of customer who isn't loyal at all. This new customer will go to the newest player, the oldest player, the lowest price, the highest price, and maybe even back to you…you, who had all along been counting them as your loyal customers.

Just as TV viewers zap their way through a 500-station electronic universe, customers now switch brands, switch stores, buy by mail, buy foreign, or stop buying altogether. And so, from the comfortable cocoons of old predictable consumer behaviour, has emerged the Butterfly Customer. If you want to survive in the era of Butterfly Customers, the place to start is with understanding their behaviour.

THE EIGHT CHARACTERISTICS OF THE BUTTERFLY CUSTOMER

We have listened to and observed thousands of Butterfly Customers and find they have eight distinguishing traits:

1. They accept your invitation to be loyal.
2. They move across market segments.
3. They are intelligent, educated, and informed.
4. They are cynical and sceptical.
5. They would rather switch than fight.
6. They are endlessly interested in the experiences of others.
7. They are not embarrassed to be Butterflies.
8. They know their own worth.

Let's look at each trait in more detail.

They Accept Your Invitation to Be Loyal

The Butterfly Customer willingly joins your customer reward program, and those of two or three of your competitors. Companies claim to have thousands, and even millions, of so-called loyal customers on their mailing lists, gathering their points, ready to claim their rewards, and they are spending in excess of 10 billion dollars a year wooing this so-called loyalty.

But the result of this massive investment is a frenzied game in which the loyalty-program customer soon becomes an expensive liability, not the asset you thought you were paying for. Yes, they carry your laminated card and yes, they come back from time to time. But take a closer look. It's not just your loyalty or reward card they carry, it's those of your competition as well. Between us, we have 15 frequent flyer programs representing companies that spend hundreds of dollars a year to "reward" us with newsletters we don't read and special coupons we never use.

There is a gap between acceptance of the loyalty invitation and the behaviour of a truly loyal customer. Zellers, a Canadian discount chain, claimed 8 million frequent-shoppers in the Club Z loyalty program in 1994. But membership in the club was no guarantee against formidable competition. In 1993, the year before Wal-Mart purchased Woolworth Canada Inc., "Zellers posted a juicy profit of $256 million. In 1994 Zellers' earnings dipped for the first time in a decade, to $216 million, and its market share began to erode...in 1995 profit fell more than 50% to $107 million, the lowest since 1987." [1]

So while you are spending dollars in order to count a customer as loyal, so is your competitor. And, what's more, even if these customers on your database or in your reward program *are* claiming their tenth cup of coffee or cashing in those points for a free trip or using your catalogue for purchases, all you have learned is that this customer is a repeat customer—whether this Butterfly is loyal is another thing altogether.

---

[1] Brian Hutchinson, "Is this any way to run a discount store? *Canadian Business Magazine*, September 1996.

They Move Across Market Segments

The Butterfly Customer has absolutely no regard for the psycho-graphic or demographic profiles you have so carefully construct-ed. Once upon a time the certain fact that every year everyone gets a year older did tell business everything they needed to know about how consumers would behave. The predictable migratory journey through the stages of life made it easy for everyone from a department store to an automobile manufacturer to convert brand loyalty into a lifetime of purchases. At General Motors the products, from a Chevy through to a Cadillac, guided the family from its first, and probably used, car to a luxury vehicle which proclaimed one's station in life.

But when first-time mothers in their forties are common-place, when 55-year-olds at the peak of their careers are down-sized out of a job, and retirees are too busy raising their grand-children to take cruises, then all the predictors guaranteed by those old demographic models go out the window.

The 56-year-old male customer who stands in line at the bar-gain store to save a buck on a package of sport socks is the same one who purchased a $700 tuxedo in a high-end fashion store. He lunches on a two-dollar meal in the food court and then uses his new cell phone in his eight-year-old car to phone his three-year-old daughter.

How can the service sector cater to this chameleon-like cus-tomer? How can we predict what he is going to need or want next? The answer is, we can't. It's almost impossible to predict, and even more difficult to track, the behaviour of this new Butterfly Customer.

They Are Intelligent, Educated, and Informed

This may be the first generation of customers to know as much about your business as you do, and probably some things you would rather they didn't. This customer has travelled the world in fact or fantasy and has an image of service created from a myriad of locations and environs. Your customer knows that in Japan, shoppers are welcomed to the department store with a bow and that in North America every pizza company has a database of customer preferences. This customer knows what your competition is offering either by experiencing it personally, through word of mouth, movies, literature, television, or by surfing the Internet.

The Butterfly can compare prices in seven different states in seven minutes and knows that in Michigan, Ford is offering a rebate but not next door in Ontario. This customer knows what you believe in, whether you are a good corporate citizen, and what charity, if any, you support. This customer scrutinizes your literature, hears about you in the media, and follows your movement through the stock market.

The Butterfly Customer asks questions like no other before. From Land's End to Sharper Image, those in the catalogue business are adding more information to their publications to forestall the flood of calls requesting detailed facts and figures. The Butterfly Customer actively seeks out information designed to assist in decisions of whether or not to do business with you. And that information is no longer the domain of the educated, the elite, the powerful, or the rich. It is now the common currency of all customers and used to their own advantage by Butterfly Customers.

They Are Cynical and Sceptical

There's a paradox. While the Butterfly Customer wants lots of information about you, and expects you and your staff to be able to provide it, they are sceptical and mistrustful of most of what you tell them.

Once upon a time consumers believed the ads. They trusted the symbols and rarely questioned the claims made. But today's customer has withdrawn behind a curtain of scepticism, taking every promise you make with a grain of salt. Even as they doubt the truthfulness of your offer, they rarely bother to tell you. And that presents a real problem for those in charge of communications.

The gap between what customers say to researchers and what they actually do has caused more than a few companies grief when it comes to mounting a consumer advertising campaign. The head of research of a major North American manufacturer once told us, "I have stopped using consumer focus groups altogether. There are just too many customers telling us what they think we want to hear. They don't seem to care about helping us improve our product or service."

In the retail sector, stores are resigned to spending more dollars for less sales results. Once sure-fire promotional winners such as Two-for-One, today barely create a blip in the weekly sales statistics. The Butterfly Customer is not only sceptical of, but also increasingly unresponsive to, once compelling pitches.

They Would Rather Switch than Fight

Between the trusting and carefree image of television's "Happy Days" and the cynicism of today's "Seinfeld" lie three decades of aggressive consumer action. Starting in the late sixties, if consumers found you wanting, they told you about it. These visible and vocal customers were fighting back, interested in change and eager to let you know if you had messed up. From boycotts led by Ralph Nader and Caesar Chavez to the popular *Consumer Report* magazine, customers were encouraged to display assertive and even aggressive behaviour to direct business to change its ways—or else!

Perhaps the epitome of this behaviour is the vigilante customer. First widely described by Faith Popcorn in the 1991 bestseller,

The Popcorn Report,[2] this customer was out there in your place of business telling you what they wanted, fighting for their rights, and expecting you to change your business to suit their needs. Their message to business was crystal clear. Clean up your act or watch helplessly as your competition reaped the spoils of switched loyalties.

But the fight has gone out of the Butterfly Customer. This is a tired consumer who, when invited to "Tell the president about your experience," increasingly has no interest in responding. From 1989 to 1996 we have watched the "nothing to say" response rise from 7% to 18%. Customers reply to the follow-up question, "Why not?" with variations on the theme, "Why bother, no one's listening anyway." The current reduction in customer complaints has less to do with a great improvement in service than it does with a collective shrug. What energy the Butterfly Customer does have is devoted to switching, not fighting.

They Are Endlessly Interested in the Experiences of Others

For as long as we can remember, word of mouth and personal references have been the most valuable form of information and influence on your customer. From a 1981 Whirlpool Corporation consumer survey to a 1996 International Data Corporation report, researchers report that "friends" rank higher than anything else when it comes to trusted sources for advice on what to purchase.

The consumer, always wary of the ulterior motives inherent in your recommendations, more than ever seeks to access unbiased sources. And today they can search far beyond the backyard fence for advice and information. At least in the old days, if your customers were going to get information from their friends or

---

[2] Faith Popcorn, *The Popcorn Report: Faith Popcorn on the Future of Your Company, Your World, Your life* (New York: Doubleday Currency, 1991).

neighbours, you could count on the fact that the friend giving the advice lived in the same area and shared the same experiences of your operation as your customer. No longer.

The World Wide Web offers instant access to "friends" who are remarkably influential, and entirely outside the control of your business. Imagine! The sceptic, always on guard against your ulterior motive, now has the ability to talk to total strangers who can strongly influence their buying decisions. Through access to the Internet, the Butterfly Customer can investigate, evaluate, decide, and act based on the experience of others half a world away. They have the chance to receive more pure, unfiltered data with which to make their decision than any other customer before them. Counting on the kindness of strangers to provide counsel and guidance is a way of life for the modern consumer.

They Are Not Embarrassed to Be Butterflies

Today's customers are unashamed of their Butterfly behaviour. The personal consequences that might have once embarrassed the customer who was tempted to stray just aren't there any more. It's not like the old days when relationships were maintained because the customer and storekeeper knew they would be seated beside each other in church next week and a change in patronage would make for an uncomfortable encounter.

The explosion of choices of where to shop, eat, and even pray, has provided a cloak of anonymity under which Butterfly Customers can easily disappear as they flit from store to store and from service to service. They know they can go anywhere they wish, to any other provider they wish, and that they really do have control. This is the customer who, without a second thought, abandons merchandise in the middle of the store if they feel they have been kept waiting too long. This is the customer who won't stand in line when there are ten other options on the way home.

They are the ones who boldly suggest a discount for cash. And it is this customer who tells you to your face that they are going to do some price comparisons at your competition and you'll hear from them later...maybe.

Today's customer who flits from one good deal to another, is thought to be a "smart" consumer. They are not ashamed of their behaviour and have no guilt about being a Butterfly Customer.

They Know Their Own Worth

Butterfly Customers have heard how important they are to your business. They may even have read the same books on service that sit on your bookshelf. Butterfly Customers know they are worth their weight in gold to you. They know that you want them as a loyal repeat customer, and exactly what that's worth to your business. Butterfly Customers understand their value, even if it sometimes appears that business doesn't. Don't forget how much information this consumer has. They have heard how much damage one dissatisfied customer can do to an organization. They know that while the choices in the service sector have been growing in leaps and bounds, the customer base has been shrinking.

These new Butterfly Customers are valuable and ready to remind you of that fact...just in case you forget.

A NEW BREED OF CUSTOMER

From the cocoon of customers, who at every rite of passage from back-to-school to baby showers, came back to the tried and familiar, has emerged a complex new customer who is always on the move.

It's a wonderful time to be a Butterfly as retailers and service providers everywhere strive to entice this elusive new breed of customer. Every day customers are bombarded with new concepts, new products, and new services to try. And there are sales and special offers galore, all designed to lure prospective buyers from retailer to retailer, from bank to bank, from credit card to credit card, and from brand to brand looking to see what's new, what's better, what's different.

This ever-changing face of the marketplace has contributed to the creation of the Butterfly Customer whose *first* instinct is to try something new, something better, something different, and whose *last* instinct is to stay loyal to any one offer.

These are the customers you must persuade to be faithful to your business. You must persuade them to be constant in their behaviour—buying your service, patronizing your store or restaurant, or flying your airline. Business survival depends on a base of faithful and constant customers, on customer loyalty.

THE SEARCH FOR ELUSIVE CUSTOMER LOYALTY

Thousands of companies have become frustrated—and less profitable—as they turn their structure and personnel inside out to try to satisfy, delight, and wow the Butterfly Customer, only to find the rewards fleeting and elusive. And yet, despite the difficulty and expense, feats of superhuman service have somehow become the goal of every company and the driving force of modern customer service.

Why? Because over the last "service excellence" decade we have become captive to some widely held misconceptions about service and how to leverage its value to build loyalty with the Butterfly Customer.

The Rise of the Service Excellence Myth

Since Tom Peters first burst on the scene and took us all (although some of us reluctantly) on a *Search for Excellence* in

1982, the business world has been turning itself inside out trying to find the secret of customer loyalty. This fifteen-year endeavour may well turn out to be one of the most *costly* crusades of all time.

Like the quest to find the Holy Grail, the search for customer loyalty took on a life of its own and the mission became almost more important than its objective. How did so many businesses get caught up in this incredible quest—spending millions in hot pursuit of the Grail which only appeared to be more elusive the harder we tried?

The Service Pendulum

As consumers began to behave more and more like Butterflies, business quickly reacted. Questions were asked, hypotheses built, and solutions proffered. Pundits and researchers argued that, all things being equal, service was *the* factor that would determine customers' perception of value. And so the drive to deliver superhuman feats of service began.

Perhaps it was described best as the "moment of truth"[3] when business realized it took only a service nanosecond to build, or destroy, valuable lifetime relationships. Those in charge also thought one didn't have to wait a lifetime to evaluate success in achieving the goal of loyal customers. If customers returned more often the business would know it had succeeded in the search for loyalty.

A myriad of creative, imaginative, exciting, and expensive reward programs were developed and put into place to lure the customer to be loyal. But despite all the efforts, the service sector watched helplessly as customers lost interest and flitted off to try the latest, greatest, newest, cheapest, biggest...somewhere else.

Manufacturers became slaves to the mantra of Total Quality

---

[3] Jan Carlzen, *Moments of Truth*, HarperCollins, 1989.

Management, only to be hit with declining market share and sinking stock prices as the high investment required to please a customer was rewarded with clients who still didn't think twice about taking hard-earned brand loyalty to the competition.

Shareholder equity now became the rallying cry and in boardrooms everywhere the message became—cut costs! And so, like the Queen of Hearts in Alice, we heard the service sector shouting "Off with their heads" while engaging in the worst example of corporate bulimia ever seen. After years of bingeing on unskilled and untrained employees to deliver service, the '90s brought a cycle of purging which resulted in staff layoffs unequaled since all the female workers left the factories and went home at end of the Second World War.

WHERE IS BUSINESS TODAY?

As the cost-cutting approach to building profits reaches its inevitable nadir, the search to add value and build loyalty is once again at the forefront.

Loyal customers…attract them, steal them, reward them, but whatever it takes…get them. Business is using many different methods to attract and retain customers. Here is one:

> *"Warm Fuzzies," was the response to our question regarding what the company was doing to improve customer service. The Vice-President went on to explain that each employee was challenged to provide every customer with at least one warm fuzzy during every interaction: a smile, a compliment, or a candy from the bowl on the counter.*

Warm fuzzies are best suited to kids' pajamas and what Butterfly Customers really want is substance and lasting value. But at least this company had implemented a service practice that was relatively benign. While it didn't make much of a positive impression on the Butterfly, at least it did no permanent damage either.

BUTTERFLY NETS

In an attempt to capture customer loyalty, members of the service sector began to set traps for the Butterfly. Out came the nets created around boardroom tables and off they went running. But the nets developed by business over the last decade to try and capture the elusive Butterfly should be illegal and, if the customer were chairman of the board, they would be. Here are two examples customers tell us they hate the most.

Reward and Loyalty Programs

Why are retailers and service businesses all over the continent trying to control the customer's buying habits by attaching them to their company with artificial threads? Some call them customer loyalty programs, others refer to them as customer reward programs, but the customers see them for what they are—Golden Handcuffs. It's critical that implementers of these programs remember that even though the handcuffs may be golden, they still chafe the customer.

Where are these programs? Well just take a look in your wallet, and count all the cards which proclaim you as a loyal customer of some establishment or other. These aren't reward programs, they are a blatant form of hostage taking. Here's one recent experience that left us so excited we can't wait to tell you about it.

> *Double park, run into a busy pet food store in an out-of-the-way neighbourhood. Spend $2.40 on a couple of cans of designer cat food. The clerk ignores other waiting customers to waste precious minutes handing out and explaining in lengthy detail the store's loyal customer card, explaining,*

"present this card at every purchase and once you reach $200 you will get a $10 credit towards your next purchase."

Wow! This means that for the next two years we have to drive out of our way, carry this card around with us, remember to present it when we shop here, and for all that effort on our part, we'll get a discount of less than 5%! Excuse me, this is the '90s. Does anyone do anything for a 5% discount? And, if we're the ones being rewarded, how come we're doing all the work?

Even successful programs that offer the customer real value, such as those offered by the airlines, are getting so diluted they have added level after level of reward: level one, gold, platinum, Presidents Club, and on and on. The resulting complexity siphons valuable profit dollars into technology to track consumer behaviour and program maintenance, for no appreciable corporate benefit.

We're sure you belong to several of these programs but has anyone ever asked you whether it had an influence on your purchase patterns? Of the 350 consumers we interviewed in the spring of 1996, not one could recall being asked such a question by any one of the suppliers of the 856 cards they carried in their collective wallet.

More and more we see clients kneeling down in front of the information idol, spending thousands, hundreds of thousands and, in some cases, millions of dollars in hardware and software designed to "capture" customer information and manage loyalty programs. But they aren't loyalty programs, they are only programs designed to track repeat customer behaviour.

Automatic Renewals

In the drive to get the loyal customer count up (customer retention, repeat visits, etc.) companies looked for a quick and easy way to earn positive numbers. And they found one—don't ask the customer if they are loyal, just *assume* they are. Record clubs, cable companies, and credit cards are especially guilty of the venal sin of ensuring "loyalty" through an assumptive sale.

Credit card companies automatically include next year's fee on the bill in the smug belief they have already earned next year's loyalty. Not only do they fail to seek permission to continue the relationship, they make the process of reversing the annual fee just difficult enough that all but the most disgruntled customers will let it slide. The customer complaints we hear about the effort to cut the card up and then get the fee back have less to do with the few dollars involved than with the insult that "this company thinks I am their property." The Butterfly Customer chooses where they will do business.

In Canada, the cable industry changed its billing procedures forever when a negative billing practice that had been the industry standard for years finally caused a nation-wide revolt in 1995. Customers in droves, refused to pay for a service they had not actively selected. Never again will cable companies assume that customers have purchased a service unless they actively take the initiative to cancel it.

Even book-of-the-month and record clubs are having to rethink the practice of saying that even though you didn't order it, we sent it to you, so you own it, and you have to pay for it. No business can assume that customers who have paid a bill they did not ask for or taken possession of a product they did not actively buy, are loyal. And for heaven's sake, don't count them as such.

Other Nets

If you want to know how many nets are in use in your organization, simply list all your offers, practices, or policies designed to create loyalty and then evaluate them as value to the customer versus value to your company. Here are some common ones.

OBJECTIVE: To evaluate the use of nets in your organization.

PROCESS: Gather all the ways in which you encourage customers to return to do business with you. For each one evaluate how much it benefits you versus how much it benefits your customers.

For instance, if customers need to make purchases before they get their "reward," what percentage of savings on discount will it represent? How much work does the customer have to do (e.g., remember the card, ask at the cash, etc.)? Does the activity add time to the transaction? Remember those time-poor consumers.

Gather together some customers or staff and ask them to complete the same exercise.

TACTIC: Ask those who serve the customers which programs they would drop and why. They know what customers really say and do at the cash desk.

Putting a customer on a mailing list without their permission or, even worse, selling that list to a third party. Share and share alike doesn't apply when it comes to the names and profiles of your customers.

Collecting information about the customer and using it without their permission. The jeweller who called to thank Mrs. Jones for an expensive purchase which her husband had made and given to someone else learned that lesson too late.

Selling the customer what they don't want in order to fix your inventory mistakes. The Butterfly Customer understands that

*the "free with purchase" bonus is often a way for a business to
reduce excess inventory or capacity, rather than a genuine gift.*

Whenever there is more value to your company than to the
customer, be careful, it may be a net. What you perceive as something designed to garner customer loyalty, the Butterfly Customer
perceives as just one more annoyance, or worse, a lure into a trap.

Can the Butterfly Customer Ever Be Loyal?

Before you start on yet another ill-fated search, you first need to
learn to live with the Butterfly Customer. Will they ever give up
the glamour, the excitement, the lure of being able to flit from
place to place?

To understand the potential for loyalty, we looked at the cause
of Butterfly behaviour. Even as the customer accepts the loyalty
card they will never use, reads the fine print on every garment
tag, tries every new store at least once, how are they feeling?

When we examined the emotional subtext, we quickly discovered that what's really going on here is not only about choice.
Even in the 1950s when department stores such as Eaton's in
Canada and Sears in the United States had two-thirds of every
consumer dollar, customers could have chosen other retailers. It
isn't about being better educated, or plugged into consumer experiences half a world away. It's not about being in demand, or
being able to be anonymous. These are all outcomes, descriptions
of the behaviour, not reasons for it.

So, what is it that underlies the emergence of this Butterfly
behaviour? At the heart of the transformation from a loyal customer
who thought of your offer first, into a Butterfly who doesn't think of
you twice, is one thing, and one thing only—a decline in trust.

CHAPTER TWO

Breaking Trust With the Customer

SOME READERS MIGHT be uncomfortable right about now. After all, this is a book about building loyalty and profits. What do business topics like that have to do with the emotional subject of whom customers trust?

To see, come with us on a brief journey to test your own trust quotient.

THE TRUST FACTOR

We began pursuing trust as an explanation of Butterfly behaviour as a result of a pattern that emerged from hundreds of adjective checklists completed by customers. The adjective checklist is a simple and commonly used approach to illuminate customer perceptions. In response to carefully devised questions, customers check every adjective which they feel describes a certain product or experience.

At first, trust was just one of the 50 words on the alphabetical list. That is, until an interesting pattern began to emerge as we worked with the data, cross-tabbing adjectives to customer behaviour and intent. "Trust" was checked in virtually every instance where the customer also demonstrated loyal behaviour. They not only returned often, they actively referred their friends and were even willing to pay a little extra for the relationship. Now that's a loyal customer!

And, the adjective trust was conspicuously absent from customer answers describing service providers which they didn't patronize nearly as often and to which they virtually never referred friends. Paying extra didn't even enter into the equation for this group.

Years in the business had taught us that 100% of consumers never agree on anything. So we ran the data set one more time and still found that 100% of 236 female customers had selected trust as an attribute of the perfect store when it comes to shopping for technology. Male shoppers were not far behind; of 287 interviewed, 96% had the word trust on their list.

About the same time, the word trust began surfacing more frequently in focus groups as well. Respondents were talking about trust, unprompted. They not only used the word but went on to place value on it, describing it in almost wistful terms.

"I want to be able to trust they are always going to have the special—even when I shop late Saturday afternoon."

"It's hard to trust someone who doesn't know the first thing about the product they are selling."

"It would be really nice not to have to spend all that time checking my credit card slips to make sure I received all my airline points."

What was going on? Why was trust both apparently at the root of loyalty and a scarce commodity? We soon began to believe a lack of trust was everywhere and with everyone.

Want some proof of that broad statement? Test your own personal trust quotient.

WHO DO YOU TRUST?

Quickly review the following list and mark your level of trust as defined by the Oxford Dictionary: *Firm belief that this person or thing may be relied upon.*

Government Effectiveness			Safety of Our Streets		
High	Medium	Low	High	Medium	Low
Accuracy of the Media			**Honesty of Other Citizens**		
High	Medium	Low	High	Medium	Low
Safety of Our Children			**Objectivity of Police**		
High	Medium	Low	High	Medium	Low
Clergy as Role Model			**Corporations Act Responsibly**		
High	Medium	Low	High	Medium	Low
Companies Invest in the Future			**Life Will be Better Next Year**		
High	Medium	Low	High	Medium	Low
Politicians Keep Their Promises			**Schools to Educate Children**		
High	Medium	Low	High	Medium	Low

So how many "Highs" did you score? In how many instances do you have a firm belief on which you would rely?

We have given this survey to thousands of people: respondents in focus groups, workers in various service sectors, and

executives of multinationals. They all find surprisingly few institutions worthy of a high score. This simple trust quotient exercise
quickly and effectively helped us understand the lack of trust
with which customers approach each interaction.

So now we had a correlation between customers choosing to
do business with a company and trust. And, we found that in general, trust is scarce. The next step was to delve even deeper. Was
this a new phenomenon, or was it a situation which has always
existed? After all, we were seeking to understand this Butterfly
Customer. Was there a difference in the levels of trust from the
days of loyal customer behaviour to now? Could that be the explanation of this new customer that service providers were seeing
everywhere?

ARE TRUST LEVELS DECLINING?

Certainly since Og roamed the earth, club always at the ready,
there have been people who would be what we call "low trusters,"
but a quick look at the literature uncovers a disturbing trend.
Looking back at the '50s, we see what was once almost a univer-
sal willingness to believe in institutions, mutate into today's cynicism and mistrust.

LYING

Everybody's Doin' It
(Honest)

Time magazine cover of October 1992.

This was *Time* magazine's cover in the middle of the Bush–
Clinton election. You remember, that was back when Bush's
famous "Read My Lips" and Clinton's, "I didn't inhale" statements

resulted in the *Time*/CNN poll reporting only 14% of the respondents believing there was more honesty in government today than ten years ago. This was a further decline from 33% in 1978 and 80% in 1956.

So what has happened in the past half-century to cause this dramatic decline? This was more than the legacy of Richard Nixon. "This is a collective belch of a society choking on misrepresentation, dishonesty, and a devaluation of core values."[1]

Mistrust has engulfed us. We left our children in the care of friendly, kindly caregivers only to find they were abusive. We counted on the fairness of law enforcement officers until we saw the Rodney King tapes. We relied on the Red Cross to provide pure products until they were charged with continuing to distribute HIV-tainted blood long after experts had begun ringing alarm bells.

No wonder trust today is a rare and precious commodity. The list of statements which we will accept without proof grows shorter with each passing year as we are faced with evidence that what we once held to be true must continuously be re-evaluated.

Is it any wonder that your customer has begun to display Butterfly behaviour? Can anyone blame customers for withdrawing their loyalty? No! Not at all. Who wouldn't want to put on the colourful protection of the Butterfly, never resting on anything firmly enough or long enough to be hurt? Being a Butterfly seems to be the safe thing to be.

Some of you may be tempted by the thought that business should learn to live with the Butterfly and forget about trying to return to the days of customer loyalty. After all, this loss of trust isn't really anything business could do something about. It isn't *your* fault. Or is it?

---

[1] Gemini Consulting Inc. "Transformations," 1994.

IN BUSINESS WE TRUST

Business is not immune from the general malaise and downward trend in trust. By 1989 authors were already reporting that confidence in business and business leadership was in a free fall, from a level of 70% in the late '60s to about 15% according to the authors of *The Cynical Americans*.[2] Remember those butterfly nets? Your customers have a great deal to say about what business, retail, and service providers have done that is untrustworthy. At the heart is a litany of broken promises that have caused a profound emotional reaction in the collective consumer psyche.

One of the primary ways in which business breaks promises has to do with the rise of the Customer Service Culture. Just think about some of the titles of recent bestsellers which purport to help business create, maintain, and retain loyal customers: *How to Create Loyal Customers. Positively Outrageous Service. Raving Fans. Knock Your Socks Off Service.* Customer service…customer service…customer service…book titles, training seminars, and articles abound until we're sick of hearing about it. But what has been the impact on your customer?

Over the past decades, the urban myths which have grown around miraculous feats of service have fueled the customer's expectations to unrealistic levels. We were at first astounded and then bemused by customer sophistication about the world of service. Comments like, "I want them to be more like, you know, that department store in California" showed that, although the details about Nordstroms might be sketchy, the expectation was not. When equally impressive service isn't delivered by you, your customer is disappointed and perceives that, although it was unspoken, you broke an implied promise.

---

[2] Donald L. Kanter and Philip H. Mirvis, *The Cynical Americans: Living and Working in an Age of Discontent and Disillusion* (San Francisco: Jossey-Bass, 1989).

Unrealistic Service Expectations

An independent fashion chain wanted to live out the ultimate service promise and developed a "no questions" return policy. One shopper who returned a pair of slacks with a broken zipper could have received every penny back, but chose instead to have the zipper replaced. It was, and the customer left completely satisfied.

So what's so unusual about a customer expecting a zipper to be replaced? Nothing. But later, when it was discovered that the garment was seven years old and finding a replacement zipper cost the company dearly in lost time and effort, one executive mused, "Even cars don't come with that length of warranty!"

Right, but somehow, the expectation created in this customer's mind was that this was a reasonable request. The explosion of customer expectations created by the service craze caused a reaction that added fuel to the broken-promise blaze. In an attempt to gain some protection from these escalating expectations, some consultants began advising their clients to "under promise and over deliver." Did they imagine customers wouldn't quickly recognize that approach as dishonest and just one more broken promise, perhaps even more reprehensible because of the inherent cynicism?

But being at the receiving end of broken promises isn't just an intellectual exercise. It generates a profound emotional reaction which has cost business loyalty, profits, and opportunities.

THE UH-OH FEELING

Alone in an empty subway car late at night. The seedy looking stranger who gets on at the next stop chooses to sit right next to you. Uh-oh!

A sudden lurch in the airplane comes with no warning and is followed by an instruction to do up your seat belt. Uh-oh!

It's the package wrapped in plain brown paper left on an empty seat on a bus in London. Uh-oh! Uh-oh!

A little too dramatic? Well maybe. But now you get the picture. The Uh-oh feeling is a message that is not only delivered at a conscious level by your brain but is felt in the nerves in the pit of your stomach. Your inner voice cries, "This isn't what I expected." "You have broken your promise to me." "I have no faith that I know how things will turn out."

When training small children to recognize dangerous situations, skilled psychologists focus on the Uh-oh feeling. Even the very young instinctively know when something is wrong and, once given permission to speak out, don't hesitate to identify the situation and the feeling.

Think back to the Butterfly nets discussed in Chapter One and consider them in light of the Uh-oh feeling we have just described. The very practices which are meant to increase the customer loyalty count create some of the strongest and most negative Uh-oh's when we listen to customers' innermost feelings about doing business with your business.

The customer gladly takes your loyalty card, only to find during their next visit to the store, its use adds several minutes to the transaction time. Uh-oh!

The customer responds to the invitation to a "Customer Appreciation Day" sale only to find less than 20% of the items are at a reduced price. Uh-oh!

The customer calls your 800 number for the special advertised in the morning paper only to learn that the item is no longer available. Uh-oh!

It is these Uh-oh feelings which customers describe when they recount their experiences with business. It is this feeling that in varying degrees of intensity is contributing to the erosion of trust and the resulting Butterfly behaviour.

Some of the elements which cause mistrust are out of your control. But Uh-oh feelings are not. From the 70% off "regular price" sale to the "money back guarantee," the promises of business are everywhere. If there is an absence of integrity in the delivery, then that company is playing fast and loose with customer trust.

A STRING OF BROKEN PROMISES

All too often the customer experiences a dark spot between the contract promised (either stated or implied) by a business with its customers and the reality of the service experience. Every customer in the world has, at one time or another, experienced the shadow of a broken promise. We're not just talking about dealing with those unsavory characters who purposefully set out to dupe the consumer. They will always be a part of the world, promising heaven and delivering hell every time. But beyond the shady activities of badly run businesses, customers find a dark side in some very common business practices. Join us in the shoes of the customer as they fall into the shadows of broken promises:

While the grocery retailer is basking in the light of a newly renovated store, the customer is stressed because the item that has been in the same aisle, on the same shelf, for the last twelve months has just disappeared.

While the airline is congratulating their marketing department on the promotion that increased seat sales through low fares, a last-minute trip finds a frequent-flyer business *traveller squished into a full-fare middle seat, listening to the bore in the coveted aisle seat boast about the "fantastic" $79.00 fare.*

The president of a high-profile store kibitzes with Hollywood celebrities in a fun campaign that implies glamour and star-quality attention for the customer. The reality? When the customer arrives in the store, as far as the eye can see, there is no staff, no president, no glamour, and definitely, no star-studded attention.

Service and retail businesses have created a profusion of practices which cause the Uh-oh feeling; practices that by their very nature industry insiders don't even notice. These are stories of how otherwise intelligent companies break trust with their customers. These are the fables that explain how, despite millions of dollars invested in telling consumers how terrific the shopping and service experience will be, most companies still continue to give their most valuable corporate asset, their customers, the Uh-oh feeling as they break yet another promise.

The Practice of Bait and Switch

The most heinous version—ads or special deals that draw customers to a company or into a store only to find the advertised special "sold-out" and a poor substitution in its place—has now been outlawed in many provinces and states. But more subtle variations are still an industry norm and customers hate your company for offering them and mistrust virtually all "sales" because of it.

Just walk through any mall where virtually every window is adorned with "50% off" signs. Sounds terrific until you move in for a closer look. That's when you see the teeny-tiny add-on caveats that lead you to realize that all of the store's merchandise is half-price—all except the good stuff, that is. What greets the customer in the store? A forlorn rack of picked-over sale merchandise and every other inch of space bursting with the new, not-on-sale stock.

And another Butterfly Customer is born.

Treating Customers Like Thieves

Another common practice is to tell customers your main goal is their satisfaction and then put barriers in their way. Have you ever tried to return something to one of the warehouse clubs? We did, when they sold us a phone that was defective. We obeyed the rule that stated "No returns without original packaging," and also the one about bringing back the receipt, and doing it all within ten days. What we neglected to bring was our warehouse club membership card, so we were detained at the door and forbidden entry...at least until a supervisor realized that this was a rule begging to be broken. Although we eventually received our refund, the extra time and energy invested was a strong negative influence on future purchases at warehouse clubs. The savings would have to be very significant to be worth the potential hassle.

A chain of high-end fashion stores advertises the benefit of purchasing several matched items to complete the customer's spring wardrobe. But, as every fashion shopper knows, a very common business practice will get in the way of taking advantage of this offer. The fitting room sign stating "Only three garments at a time" is strategically placed next to the one which tells the shopper that the fitting rooms are being monitored and shoplifters will be prosecuted.

Yes, there are rip-off artists out there who spend their entire lives figuring out how to beat your security system, but the vast majority of people are honest and just want what was promised.

In a time when the customer can shop by catalogue or on the Internet, why does business continue to enforce rules which work *against* the honest majority instead of *for* them?

If the dictionary phrase, "confident expectation," is the ultimate description of trust as customers would describe it, there are far too few companies that come close to delivering that feeling. Instead customers are forced to deal with companies where they never quite know if any promise, no matter how small, will be kept.

Consider these examples:

Customers who won the battle for low-fat airline meals had only a short time to relax before being bombarded with reports that some of those "low-fat" meals actually contained more calories than the regular fare.

Consumers religiously check bank statements each month because, even with some of the most sophisticated financial software in the world, deposits are mysteriously mislaid or interest credited to the wrong account.

At a time when cash payments are being phased out every-where, seniors insist on being able to pay their bills in person because "the mail can't be trusted" to deliver on time, and heaven only knows what happens to payments made at the automated teller machine.

THE HIGH COST OF LOW TRUST

So no one trusts anyone any longer. What does that have to do with customer service? With loyalty? With your ability to make a profit? After all, you are just trying to run a business, not run for public office.

The old saying "Fool me once, shame on you. Fool me twice, shame on me" is a pretty accurate description of the protective position that consumers have taken. As individuals it makes us feel stupid when we are tricked and it makes us angry at the business or institution which made us feel that way. And, if we experience too many such incidents, we enter what psychologist Julian Rotter calls a "low-trust mode."

What happens when customers enter a low-trust mode? Their behaviour is evident and easily measured. The high-trust consumer says "I will trust until given evidence that I cannot trust." The low truster says "I will not trust until given clear evidence that I can trust." To understand the additional effort required to handle the low-trust customer in both financial and productivity terms, all you need to do is to imagine yourself in the used-car business.

A surprisingly large number of consumers who say they would never trust a used-car salesperson have never, in fact, purchased a used car! How can customers be so sure of their suspicions of the used-car salesperson with absolutely no personal experience? How can people in focus groups say, "I personally haven't had any trouble" while blithely rating the overall profession negatively?

The answer? Collective memory. Some memory seems to be coded into our brains even without personal experience. This collective memory has created an environment where whole industries and professions have lost customer confidence as trust has all but disappeared and where almost every potential customer starts the relationship from a position of low trust.

For a long time now the diet industry, health and fitness clubs, auto repairs, the legal profession, and, sad to say, most of the retail sector have started altogether too many interactions from a position of low trust. And the list continues to grow with consumers adding banks, brokers, and real-estate firms to the list. More recently a large number of health-care professionals are joining this dubious club—doctors, hospitals, and health insurance "schemers" (in the words of one focus group consumer).

How is this memory created? Through experiences which are far different than those promised. Just take a look at the gap between what a composite of pharmacy ads were presenting as a factual experience to their customers and what was actually experienced at the counter. The exercise took place during a time when the industry was trying to combat the rise of telephone and other discount pharmacists. Consumers, based on current advertising promises, should have expected the following in every interaction:

- Questions about other medications currently being taken
- Questions about previous experience with the medication
- The pharmacist ensuring directions were understood
- Advice about how to use the medication
- Being called by name

In fifty "mystery shops" we heard "perfect" interactions just twice. The others ranged from getting some things right, to interactions where frankly, a faceless telephone operator would have been a dramatic improvement. The service promises were not delivered.

Every time the customer experiences an Uh-oh feeling, a little bit of their trust erodes until there is none left. When there are enough Uh-oh experiences, customer trust levels decline until even the most reputable of firms are negatively affected.

Trust is an asset of your business just like buildings, inventory, or staff. And unlike those, once lost, there is no insurance policy in the world which will guarantee its replacement.

The Rewards of Trust

"Loyal customers are won when the customers, consciously or unconsciously, judge the company to be capable of solving their problems and meeting their needs."[3]

Trust is the customer believing your business will meet their needs, consistently and with no surprises. Once the customer perceives your company is able to deliver this to them, even the Butterfly will be willing to give you its trust.

What happens when the Butterfly Customer trusts you? Is their trust manifested in their behaviour? In their attitude? What's in it for you is a loyal customer—the elusive Monarch for which all service providers search.

[3] James M. Kouses and Barry Z. Posner, *Credibility: How Leaders Gain and Lose It, Why People Demand It* (San Francisco: Jossey Bass, 1993).

CHAPTER THREE

The Return of the Monarch

THE BUTTERFLY CUSTOMER, that creature more at home in motion than at rest, is here to stay, presenting a very real challenge to business. You will have to work very hard to earn trust from this customer whose first response to any plea for loyalty is suspicion and cynicism. The old triggers of habit, convenience, or even lowest price won't work. But the effort must be made, because the rewards of converting the flitting Butterfly into the loyal Monarch are too great to ignore.

THE FIVE CHARACTERISTICS OF THE MONARCH

The Monarch is still a butterfly. The characteristics we described in Chapter One still describe them. They are intelligent, curious, suspicious, and know their own worth. But the Monarch is a species of butterfly which, despite taking various byways and pathways, can be counted upon to return to the familiar on a regular basis.

These loyal Monarch Customers are less expensive to attract. It usually doesn't take an extensive advertising campaign or give-away promotion to entice them back to your business. They take less transaction time from your staff and are quicker to buy because they are less sceptical and don't need a large amount of convincing. They are more willing to pay list price and are less price sensitive all around.

But how do they behave? How can you and your front-line staff recognize these valuable customers? Here are the contrasting behaviours of the Monarch Customer and how you can recognize one.

1. Monarchs always return—sooner or later!
2. Monarchs often send someone in their place
3. Monarchs always have an opinion
4. Monarchs share their homework
5. Monarchs are forgiving and giving

Monarchs Always Return—Sooner or Later!

It may take a while but sooner or later the Monarch returns. That customer coming up to the counter that you recognize but haven't seen for quite some time may be one of that loyal flock, not because of the uncertain enticement of some reward card in their wallet, but of their own volition.

The shame here is that staff in the service sector never seem to stay in one place long enough to recognize returning customers. Isn't it infuriating that just as the teller at the bank or the flight attendant on the shuttle gets to know you, they disappear?

If you want to find out if you have Monarchs among your customers there are two things you can do. First, do everything possible to keep the same staff on the same regular routines. You want the occasional visitor to feel as if they never left! Second, be sure *all* staff are trained to welcome returning customers, asking them the appropriate questions and enticing them to stick around long enough to gain some perspective. Not only will Monarchs get the important message, "We're so glad to see you again," your company could learn invaluable information about where your Monarchs go when they leave you and what brings them back.

Monarchs Often Send Someone in Their Place

In a recent issue of *The Service Report*, a newsletter we publish several times a year, we talked about a restaurant called Sign of the Dove in New York City to which we give our loyalty. Do we eat there every time we're in New York? Nope! During a six month period we ate at fourteen other New York eateries. So how could we be loyal? Easy! We wrote the Sign of the Dove up twice (now three times), sent them a customer who held their wedding reception there, and referred several clients, colleagues, and friends. So while we haven't personally been there in over a year, we are and should be counted as loyal customers.

How much business have you done as a result of a referral from a loyal but absent customer? If the second sign that you are enjoying the loyalty of the Monarch is that they refer others to your business, how do you recognize and how do you count the number of your goodwill ambassadors?

You could survey customers to find out how and why they decided to choose your place of business. Aaarrgghhhh...another survey. You could commission some focus groups of new customers to determine if they were referred. *Very* costly. The best and cheapest answer is to make it the responsibility of your staff (the ones you are already paying) to get this information for you and then give them the skill to ensure they can. Asking every customer how they came to choose you and what they say to others about you lets you track the Monarchs in your customer pool.

Monarchs Always Have an Opinion

If the fickle Butterfly Customer would rather switch than fight, the loyal customer often demonstrates a willingness to duke it out.

If you have customers pointing out little mistakes, telling your staff when they think something is inappropriately priced or that the service stinks, look closer. You may be hearing the beating wings of the mighty Monarch.

Loyal customers feel a sense of ownership and attachment to your business and are therefore motivated to make it better. Loyal customers are committed to you. They believe you should be in business and have a right to make a profit. They tell you when things go wrong and offer suggestions for improvement. "We're here for a long time," they seem to be saying, and so they want to contribute to ensuring you stay around.

Their "complaints" may at first appear trivial and bothersome and, in some companies a lack of understanding of the value of this customer causes those in charge, or on the front line, to turn a deaf ear and blind eye to the input. Having had their comments and suggestions rebuffed, the loyal customer leaves and you lose more than just today's sale. If you want to reward this Monarch behaviour, ensure your staff and system are set up to provide feedback on what happened to every complaint, not only in terms of how it was resolved, but also in terms of what effect it is having on your business practices.

Monarchs Share Their Homework

All Butterfly Customers are curious and informed. The difference is Monarch Customers freely offer, without prompting, information on what your competition is doing. Remember, the Monarch is still enjoying the variety and excitement of the market place.

But the loyal customer synthesizes those experiences through the filter of the companies they love the best. When they return to you, however infrequently, they have information to share.

The signal that your proportion of Monarchs is on the rise are staff who report on the details of the competition or are filled with ideas about new products and services because they are hearing about them from customers. Of course, for that to happen, staff must have the time to listen and the skill to do it effectively. If your front line does not know how to translate the information or what to do with it, you have let a valuable asset go to waste.

Monarchs Are Forgiving and Giving

Monarch customers have a remarkable tolerance for the sheer ordinariness of service life. They know the coffee won't always be exactly the right temperature and even the perkiest of airline attendants sometimes has a bad day. Customers who are loyal put elasticity in their transactions with you. They allow you to screw up once in a while and often even pitch in to help when the going gets rough.

When the Tattered Cover, a Denver bookstore was faced with a move to their new location, a couple of hundred customers volunteered to help transport a quarter of a million books. Some of them probably hadn't bought anything in over a year and would have been purged from the "loyal" customer list of many stores. But just think of the cash value of the gift these customers gave to a store that had earned their loyalty.

If your staff hear customers offer to help bag the merchandise because the store is busy, or serve themselves so staff can take care of another customer, you may be hearing the sounds of the Monarch.

OBJECTIVE: To evaluate the number of Monarch Customers in
    your business.

PROCESS: Share the profile of the Monarch Customer with
    your staff. Ensure they understand it is their job to be
    observing these behaviours as they serve customers.

TACTIC: Create a set of questions appropriate to your busi-
    ness to get staff actively tracking Monarch behaviour. For
    example: Where else have you found this service or prod-
    uct? What do those companies do better?

Think about your own behaviour. Who are the service
providers who have earned your loyalty? What about the dentist
who always keeps you waiting yet you go back time and time
again; the hairdresser or barber that you go out of your way to visit;
the airline or hotel chain you always try to use, and not for the
points. All of these are examples of loyal behaviour. We just have
to make it everyone's job to look for them and train our staff in the
skills they will need to track it, encourage it, and reward it.

There are a large number of Butterflies who would instantly
exchange their random travels for the certain pathways of the
Monarch, if only we would recognize that the true attraction for
the Monarch is not the most vivid colour or aromatic perfume—
those are everywhere—but the element which is least found in
the modern consumer garden—Trust.

CAN YOU EARN THE CUSTOMERS TRUST?

So, when there are so many broken promises in the world, what
chance does your fashion chain, restaurant, or product brand
have to earn trust from the Butterfly Customer?

You have two factors in your favour. First, there is a strong human instinct to trust. Second, customers are tired of the cost of mistrust. Customers are exhausted and resent having to expend valuable personal energy, time, and money always looking over their collective shoulder because they can't trust business to deliver what it promises.

A Strong Human Instinct for Trust

The behaviour of a newborn suggests that the desire to trust is a part of human nature. But from the day the corner store owner gave us only four candies instead of five, through to buying our first home and being surprised by all the closing costs the agent had neglected to mention, we learned that it was foolish to trust too freely. Experience after experience, year upon year, we increased our guard, became more vigilant, and developed into low trusters.

But deep down, it is trust we crave. As hard as it is to be trusting in today's world, we want to believe the best.

Kathie Lee Gifford (of the Regis and Kathie Lee fame), an outspoken opponent of unfair labour practices, and Wal-Mart, an icon of down-home, Southern honesty and trust, came together in an incident in the summer of 1996.

Just blocks from the studio where Kathie Lee tapes her daily show, employees (mostly illegals) in a sweatshop were working slave-labour hours without pay to meet a deadline on an order of Kathie Lee blouses destined for Wal-Mart.

The day this story hit the media, we did a telephone poll of customers. A sample of the questions and responses demonstrate both the ingrained cynicism and inherent instinct to trust of Butterfly Customers.

Q: Did either of the two main parties know this practice was going on?

A: "How can you make and sell a blouse at $9.99 any other way?
Wal-Mart makes more than half of the selling price, Kathie Lee
makes money for putting her name on it so that leaves how much
for making the product? Anyone can see it's not possible without
screwing somebody, but I'd like to believe they didn't know."
"Well, I guess it's hard to know everything that goes on in business."

Q: How does this incident make you feel as a consumer?

A: "Saddened. I really want to believe that they didn't know, but I
don't think this is the first time for Wal-Mart"
"It will make me question Kathie Lee's credibility from now on."
"It just goes to show...you can't trust anyone anymore."

On the one hand Butterflies cynically believe the partners
must have known, or were fools not to. On the other hand the
Monarch wants to believe the best of those it has come to trust.
For the record, Wal-Mart issued a statement taking responsibility for the problem and fired the manufacturer who "was in viola-
tion of a strict vendor agreement." Kathie Lee sent her husband
over to the shop with cash for the employees, and in a press con-
ference, vowed to wage war against sweatshops.

What this means for your business is that there is an opportunity to tap into our primal need...to trust. But is it enough? Is
it enough that customers want to trust? Maybe not, but there is
something else at work on your behalf. Not only is it the customer's natural instinct to trust but they also yearn for the benefits they can receive from a trusting relationship.

Tired of the Cost of Mistrust

Think about your mom shopping in any major mall today. She will
be on constant red alert to ensure she doesn't end up as an unwill-
ing participant in some random act of violence. She will scrutinize

tags and labels with diligence because the product knowledge and recommendations received from staff have to be taken with a grain of salt. She must remember which stores have "sales" with prices that are truly lower and never, ever forget to present her loyalty card for the appropriate rewards. She will question return policies, count her change twice, and check the amount on her credit card slips, all the while, guarding her purse and packages.

She will come home exhausted and frustrated by all the extra work required on her part merely to protect herself in an untrustworthy world. And it isn't over yet. She has to store the proof of purchase receipts for safekeeping to match against the frequent shopper points statement when it arrives weeks later, or in the event the product proves defective.

This burden of constant vigilance is making customers weary and the act of keeping one's mind and body on edge is exhausting. Muscles tense, adrenalin pumps, and hormone production increases as an individual prepares for the fight-or-flight response. The sheer exhaustion of maintaining this stance is similar to the stress syndrome experienced by soldiers during war and more recently by inhabitants of neighbourhoods where drive-by shootings are the norm and safety is a stranger.

Surely we aren't comparing a shopping experience to soldiering in Viet Nam or running the gauntlet in a street-gang infested housing development? Maybe we are. The intensity may be different, but the outcome is the same.

Older consumers who know they used to be able to score lots of highs on the trust quotient exercise we introduced in Chapter Two, find themselves unwillingly adopting a set of protective behaviours that require a level of emotional diligence that is exhausting. And, if you think it is bad now, just imagine today's youth as adults. If the adult consumer who grew up in trusting times has turned into a low truster, imagine what today's kids who have grown up looking over their shoulder, will be like as adults!

Is it any wonder there is a yearning for the "good old days" when one's word was one's bond? Customers want to relax both in body and mind but in order to do so, they have to find trusting environments. They want environments where they can be confident that their expectations will be delivered. No surprises, no Uh-oh feelings, and no shadows.

How Does Business Build Trust with the Butterfly?

Just as Adam Smith proclaimed, "what is scarcest is valued most,"[1] today, more than ever, customers value a trusting environment and it is in your best interest to deliver it.

We believe every business has the opportunity to tap into this yearning for the rewards of being able to trust, and when earning your customer's trust is the key to survival, this is a precious opportunity indeed.

Just as we saw with Butterfly nets, some of the practices designed to increase trust have the opposite effect. Two common ways of trying to earn trust are by using the right words and through fantastic service feats.

Can Trust Be Earned by Using the Right Words?

Will simply telling customers to trust you have the desired effect? Certainly Allstate Insurance succeeded for many years with their message that, "You're in good hands with Allstate." Or maybe it is not what is communicated but who communicates the message of trust that will be the deciding factor. Who will the Butterfly Customer believe? Is it Whoopie Goldberg for MCI, or Candace Bergen for Sprint? Companies using celebrities to deliver their messages has long been an accepted form of communicating

---

[1] Smith, Adam "The Wealth of Nations."

believability but one which has increasingly little sway over the Butterfly Customer.

And these approaches are especially unlikely to work for companies which operate in an industry which has created a collective memory of mistrust, like the automotive, pharmaceutical, banking, and government sectors. For these firms, ad campaigns saying "Trust us" or using the images of a family and its dog, have the opposite effect.

Whether industry-wide, company-wide, or product-specific, ads which promise nirvana and deliver a far different reality, exacerbate a basic lack of credibility. The faith of the customer who is the target of these ads, is further worn down. And business again fosters mistrust in the very people whose trust they would love to have.

So, telling folks you are to be trusted hardly ever works. When someone says "Trust me," the instinctive reaction is to do the exact opposite! If messages proclaiming your trustworthiness don't work the way they used to, what about delivering fantastic service? Do those companies who leap tall buildings in a single bound create trust in their customers?

Do Fantastic Service Feats Increase Trust?

Certainly many service initiatives appear to work. We all know the names of the companies that enjoyed a meteoric rise in their service image and who were cited in speeches and books everywhere. Their customers behaved like we were told loyal customers would—returning more often and sometimes referring their friends. They even sounded loyal in surveys and interviews.

But that loyalty was an illusion. Having a high number of repeat customers in the late 1980s was no guarantee for these companies against the lure of lower prices as the economy fell apart and the dollar became king.

The Gap, an often admired U.S. based casual clothing chain, experienced a 5% drop in sales in 1994. Kodak, one of Tom Peters' examples of an 1980s company which breeds productivity through people, laid off tens of thousands of workers in the following decade. Nordstroms, the service-excellence department store stalled in its growth.

If the loyal customers of these service icons, the gods of excellence, were just an illusion, what does that mean for us mere mortals in the service pantheon?

How can trust be developed by business during these most mistrusting of times? Just what can a company do to tap into the Butterfly Customer's desire to trust, to turn a roving breed into a loyal Monarch? If trust isn't earned by shouts of "Trust Me!" or from service excellence what is left? Credibility.

BE CREDIBLE IN ALL ASPECTS

To gain the customer's trust you must be credible in every aspect of your business.

- You won't build credibility if you deliver a wonderful experience at the check-in desk but give the customer the key to a dirty hotel room.
- It isn't OK to advertise the lowest price in town if the interest rate on your credit account is outrageous.
- Your published promise of expert service rings hollow when delivered by an untrained part-timer on the front line.

Customer service at its best is the delivery of a contract which is written entirely in favour of the customer. Trust is created by the consistent delivery of that contract.

What you promise—high service, self-service, phone service, drive-through service, instant service, or no service—matters less than the consistency of the match between what you deliver and what you promised in your customer contract. Trust is built when the customer never has to worry about being surprised or fooled or cheated or lied to. It's when the customer knows the product or service you offer will be as advertised. It is when the customer has a belief that what they expect will be delivered and what they are promised is an accurate representation. It is when the customer has faith, relaxes, and becomes not your vigilante adversary, but your active business partner.

To awaken the trust of the Butterfly Customer, is to awaken a sleeping giant who will bring not only the benefits of loyalty, but the gift of trust—a willingness to be a partner. Once customers start trusting you and move from low-truster to high-truster behaviour you create an environment that attracts a breed of Butterfly that every business should want—the Monarch.

Wouldn't it be a relief to not have to waste your advertising dollars to proclaim, "You can trust us" because your customers were already delivering the message on your behalf? Wouldn't it be as relaxing for you as it would be for your staff to let go of the heroic service image? Wouldn't it be wonderful to build a business which was as rewarding for your employees and your shareholders as it was for your customers, because, instead of adversaries gunning for revenge, you had partners interested in your long-term success?

Achieving the benefits of Monarch Customers is much tougher than it sounds because the customer sees and hears implied promises in all facets of your business. The advertising message you send, the quality of the product, the feel of your environment, and the policies your staff enforce all create an opportunity to build, or break, trust.

How can you create the level of credibility that attracts the Monarch? How does a business ensure the customer experience is one that fosters feelings of security? How does a business ensure that the promises made or implied can be delivered? And, how does a business experience the customer interaction in such a way as to truly gain an accurate measure of how that experience will affect customer trust?

The first step is to learn how customers experience our business offering. To do that, you need to understand the simple set of tools businesses use to create diverse experiences for their customers: the service kaleidoscope.

CHAPTER FOUR

The Service Kaleidoscope

Т HINK BACK TO when you were a kid and were given a kaleido-scope. What a wondrous thing! Put this little tube up to the light and with a simple turn of the wrist you experienced thousands of beautiful patterns and designs. Another turn and behold, another even more interesting pattern emerged. Each design appeared to be brand new, yet they were produced with the same few components. How did this thing work? Was it magic?

No, not magic, just some pieces of glass and a mirror put together in a tube. It's how they fell together that created the patterns. The components of the kaleidoscope have never changed even though today you can find fancy brass versions carrying $100 price tags.

Like the kaleidoscope, the basic components of a business do not change, but how they are placed, presented, and viewed by customers, do.

THE THREE DIMENSIONS OF THE BUSINESS KALEIDOSCOPE

A kaleidoscope has three basic components: a few pieces of coloured glass, a mirror, and a tube. And every business has three components, or dimensions, which are: the media, the physical, and the people.

Imagine! Only three components coming together in a variety of ways to create an infinite number of customer experiences and choices in retail and service businesses around the world. Millions of businesses twisting and shaking the kaleidoscope in an effort to create a myriad of choices with these three simple dimensions.

Understanding each of the three dimensions and how they work together to create so many unique experiences is the first step in understanding how to use them to build credibility with customers.

The Media Dimension

Entice, attract, provoke, invite, lure, tempt, bait. The media dimension sends the important messages to your potential customer: "Here's what we offer," "Here's how we compare to what the competition offers," or "Remember us." The ultimate goal is to incite action: pick up the phone, visit the store, ask for the product by name, buy three, buy today. These are the results sought by those who foot the advertising bill.

The media dimension includes every way a business communicates with customers: radio, television, newspaper, flyers, database marketing, telephone solicitation, signs, shelf talkers, hang tags, brochures, public relations, and many more. There are other not so obvious elements which also form part of this dimension.

Think about the name of the business as an element of the media dimension. Why are so many airlines named after countries? Perhaps they are trying to establish a sense of history and stability. And what about the role of music as part of the media message? All those retro '60s rock tunes send a subliminal message to any boomer that this is a cool product or place to shop. And let's not forget a million messages you didn't pay for, many of which you never planned to send. Because the most powerful media component of all is what customers and staff say about you to their friends—word of mouth.

The good news is that this aspect of your media dimension comes free. There is no ad agency to hire, no creative to fret over, no print to proof, no insertion costs. However, you have absolutely no control over, and sometimes no knowledge of, what is being communicated, or to whom. As a third-party endorsement, word of mouth is very credible. That is great if the message is positive—bad if it is negative.

Just think of the media dimension as anything that passively or actively, purposefully or inadvertently, overtly or covertly, communicates some expectation of your business, product, or service.

The Physical Dimension

Anything the customer tastes, touches, sees, and hears as they come into direct contact with your business is part of the physical dimension. This is perhaps the strongest and most easily understood of the three dimensions. Its elements are tangible and can be brought to the attention of the decision makers in real time and space. Kurt Salmon and Associates of New York revealed that while "service" is the proclaimed number one goal of three out of four mass market retailers, a full 68% of executive time is spent on just one dimension of the business—the physical one![1]

---

[1] Thall, et al., "A survey of Chief Executive Officers" (New York: Kurt Salmon & Associates, 1992).

Millions of dollars are spent on this dimension as designers and architects strive to create a physical manifestation of a business. It is perhaps the dimension most susceptible to fashion trends as brown shag carpet is replaced by blond wood flooring and black rubber tiles give way to Italian marble.

But it is not just the space and layout which communicate in the physical dimension. Product, packaging, and price all work together to create a powerful message to the consumer. Think about the "green" movement which enjoyed a brief burst of consumer attention in the late '80s. Packaging of many different products began to feature less exterior wrap and "natural" colours, sending the clear signal: "we're eco-friendly."

While the first two dimensions are the ones which often command the most executive attention, no company could be in business if it weren't for the third, and some think the most important dimension of all—the people dimension.

The People Dimension

The people dimension is the voice customers hear. It's the people they see and with whom they interact during their contact with your business. What is commonly called "service" forms the third dimension and success here is crucial to gaining customer trust. It is their involvement with the face or voice of your company that provides customers with the opportunity to confirm how well you do at delivering what you promise.

It's the ability of your staff to interpret your policies and procedures, to use their skills and knowledge to satisfy customer desires that, in the final analysis, makes or breaks the customer's encounter with your business. People are the transducers that take the power of the media and physical dimensions of your business and deliver them to the customer.

Without question, for most operations, this is the most difficult dimension. Ads, brochures, and signs can be created and disseminated. Physical premises, product packaging, and price can be designed, set up, and maintained. But the people represent the least controllable aspect of any service business.

THREE DIMENSIONS CREATE ENDLESS VARIETY

The media, physical, and people dimensions are the components of the service kaleidoscope. These three simple components exist in every business and are used to create a million images as companies everywhere strive to exert their power and please the customer. So how do they create such diverse experiences?

Put the service kaleidoscope up to your eye and let's take a look at the personal care products business. How many different ways can each of the three dimensions be twirled into diverse pictures? Let's take a component of each and see.

Media

A company spokesperson is a tool used by many to set up the image of the company. Watch how three companies have spun three distinct moods from promoting a company spokesperson.

The Body Shop founder Anita Roddick delivers a message of community, of nature, of healing, and how personal action and involvement can change the world. As she strides through the highlands of New Guinea for an American Express ad she sets the tone for the entire corporation.

The MAC cosmetic spokesperson couldn't be more different. At 6'4" the highly made-up transvestite RuPaul commands a different space in the popular media. This spokes "wo-man" is the bi-product's composite user.

At H$_2$0 Plus, founder Cindy Melnik personifies a personal command of business, research, and her own life in countless business magazine articles about how she reinvented a tried and true concept into a new marketing phenomenon. Crisp and technologically astute, this is a spokesperson driven by facts.

The same media tactic of a recognizable company spokesperson results in three completely different images.

Physical

The remarkable array of choice confronting the customer searching for a gift for Mother's Day illustrates the permutations possible in the physical dimension.

By the door in The Body Shop is a display of native baskets with an invitation to fill them with a personalized gift selection. Even completed gift baskets are left unwrapped, allowing each customer to decide how much packaging to use.

At MAC the product is primary. Sleek, simple, black (what else would you expect) packaging takes absolutely nothing away from the product. No frills or flounces here, even during the Mother's Day campaign.

In H$_2$0 Plus, primary-coloured, whimsical bath toys are part of every gift basket, inviting the shopper to give Mother a little treat in an otherwise busy life.

The customer in each of these physical dimensions can very quickly decide which one meets the needs or the desires of their mom.

People

What can be done to twirl the people dimension? Well, in a suburban setting where the retail staff are drawn from the same ten-mile radius, you will find more than subtle differences.

The staff members at The Body Shop are wearing a variety of comfortable, casual clothing, chatting cheerfully while answering customers' questions about the history of the product.

At the MAC cosmetic counter one is served by a staff smartly adorned in black smocks—with make-up and hair that speaks of the trendiest part of downtown. Triple earrings and even nose rings are acceptable attire here and staff can tell you which stars are using which colours in their latest movie or music video.

Over at H_2O Plus, the staff portray a far more sophisticated, business look. Staff look like the customers they serve and all model the image of the founder, Cindy Melnik.

Same candidate pool, different employee profiles. The power of the people dimension to contribute to a unique experience is evidenced one more time. Imagine the MAC staff at The Body Shop or vice versa. You can't because it doesn't fit. The three dimensions are supple tools in the hands of the creative visionary.

A 3-D World

It is easy to see the three dimensions in the world of retail. Read the flyer, look at the billboards, and listen to the radio. Take a walk through the mall and browse the windows and displays. Walk inside and talk to the people. Is every business composed of the same three dimensions with the same power to create different moods and feelings? Yes!

Think about the travel business, particularly airlines. Now there is a product which is hard to differentiate. Just how do you create a distinct image when all the airplanes are made by the same manufacturers, fly into and out of the same airport terminals, and are required to meet the same safety regulations?

Just ask Richard Branson, founder of Virgin Airlines, how he twirled the service kaleidoscope to create a media dimension

which is altogether different than that of a key competitor—
British Airways. His combination of the word virgin and the
colour pink clearly worked as he quickly grabbed a disproportionate share of the market in this highly competitive industry.

The three dimensions also apply in business-to-business
transactions. Have you had to purchase computers for your company lately? You can clearly state the differences between the
IBM and Apple product in the physical dimension. Or what about
courier companies and the people dimension? The difference
between the smartly uniformed UPS employee and the scruffy,
but fast, bicycle courier is instantly apparent.

The three dimensions are what gives a business the power to
be different, to be truly memorable for the customer, to stand out
from the crowd. And business has had a wonderful time creating
new choices for the consumer. The Butterfly Customer has never
before had so many different selections in everything from retail
to banking to soft drinks. But a creative and clever manipulation
of the dimensions does not guarantee customer loyalty. Business
also has to twirl the service kaleidoscope in a way which builds
trust.

HARMONY IN 3-D—THE KEY TO BUILDING TRUST

What creates trust for the customer is the way the three dimensions are interwoven into a seamless experience, one which is
pleasing and consistent at all levels. All of the elements of your
business working in harmony make you credible in the minds of
the customer. Credibility builds trust which in turn is the prerequisite for loyalty.

Great operations have a distinct personality which resonates
throughout the business. Where we observe customers looking
blank as they try to remember the name of the store to fill in on
the cheque they are writing, we often find that the business owner

neglected to create a distinct image that weaves through all three dimensions of the business. Maybe there is a clever use of the media dimension in the name or a newspaper ad, but the physical dimension is filled with the same old product, being sold the same old way. More often, the media and physical dimensions cleverly play off each other, but the staff display no evidence of the unique company message and are interchangeable with those of any number of competitors.

Business must learn to intertwine and seamlessly integrate all three dimensions. Let us return to the world of personal beauty care and tell the story of three companies that are rising above the competition, because of their ability to keep their kaleidoscope in sync: The Body Shop, MAC Cosmetics, and H$_2$0 Plus.

The Body Shop in 3-D

In this company the media dimension is to a large degree Anita Roddick herself. And we feel we know her as we hear stories about her efforts to source natural products and support local entrepreneurs. From the purchasing of products through native co-ops to the launching of a book that celebrates motherhood, the corporate slogan, "trade, not aid" is reinforced through the actions of the founder.

So imagine the company created by this:

- world traveller who believes in conservation,
- supporter of Amnesty International who believes that a percentage of profits must be used to aid the less fortunate,
- believer that the future of countries is cradled in the arms of its mothers.

What physical dimension would she deliver to her customers? For certain the product would be natural, incorporating ingredients that native women (and men) have been using for centuries to enhance and adorn. There would be the least amount of animal testing consistent with basic safety, with scents created from forests and fields, not laboratory test tubes. And the store environment would complete the physical experience with the use of materials, colours, scents, and lighting as natural as possible in a design which evokes the environment in a down-to-earth yet attractive way.

Finally, what about the people dimension? What would they believe? How would they demonstrate what they believed in? Well, in The Body Shop, the staff look like they use the product. They talk like they believe in the product and they spend a portion of their time contributing to charitable causes which reflect the beliefs of the company. Look in the back room of any store. Posters about charitable causes, copies of Roddick's book, *Mama Toto*, and a reminder to the staff about Earth Day indicate a pervasive corporate culture. The media persona is delivered seamlessly in the physical and people dimensions.

MAC Cosmetics

MAC had its start creating make-up for the stage, runway, and photo ops, so the selection of professional model RuPaul as key media messenger is a perfect continuation of their core values. Spokesperson Paul does interviews, works the runway at fashion launches, and doesn't hesitate to tell the world that he has been wearing make-up since he was five years old.

The physical dimension conjures up an environment designed to meet the needs of make-up professionals, complete with bright lights and minimalist packages. Product is organized as it would be in a professional's make-up case, according to colour palettes, and features all the hues found in the very latest fashion magazines.

Finally, the people dimension. Face and body adornments are the norm but don't underestimate these (mostly) young staff. They are as skilled at creating a look for the customer as they are at knowing which product to recommend. This is a company with product designed for the professional model but available to the average consumer. It's a planned and deliberate matching of all three dimensions.

H₂O Plus

In the media dimension, the founder is again a key part of the strategy, but this time the focus is on technology and research to create modern solutions. And H_2O staff are expected to grow their business through the media tactic of out-of-store presentations. Unlike Body Shop franchisees, who take their message and benefits to community groups, H_2O teams target conventions and other business groups for their sales message.

In the physical dimension, you find a modern, high-tech store where blue and green packaging and wavy window designs reinforce the image of water. Not surprisingly, all the skin care and beauty products are water-based. This is a minimalist presentation where the lines of the store are clean and crystal clear and a mineral water dispenser sits on the floor for customer convenience. Nor should one be surprised that aromatherapy herbal essences waft into the mall corridor.

And the staff? They are sleek, higher fashion, and more sophisticated than their counterparts at MAC and The Body Shop. They reflect the message sent in the media and in the physical dimensions of the business. Training focuses on developing a relationship with a customer, offering the benefits of a consistent regimen to ease the hectic life of the target customer.

The Body Shop, MAC, and H$_2$O Plus exemplify not only creative diversity through deft twirling of the service kaleidoscope, but harmony in the three dimensions. There is very little gap between what is promised (either overtly or subliminally) and what is delivered. Holistic, harmonious, seamless, and encompassing are the adjectives which describe a business where the customer basks in the light of an illuminated service experience. With so little room for doubt and discomfort, the result is that the customer can relax with confident expectation that what is expected will be delivered. As Butterfly Customers begin to trust they take on the colouration of the trusting, loyal Monarch.

THE CAUSE OF DISHARMONY

What makes the customer feel like your kaleidoscope is out of sync? What makes them shrug and flit to another store? It is when you fail to match the three dimensions. No 3-D match, no credibility. No credibility, no trust. No trust, no loyalty.

With only three dimensions, one would think it would be easy to deliver a harmonious experience to the customer and some businesses seem, instinctively, to do it very successfully. For others, cacophony better describes the result.

Disharmony often begins in the media dimension. The image you create sets up the conscious, and often more importantly, the subconscious, expectations in the mind of the customer. But at its worst, the experience rings false in every dimension.

Want evidence? Listen to one of the authors, who at this point was a fifteen-year veteran of retailing reality, describe her epiphany.

On the Beach

Daffodils were in bloom and summer not far behind the day when a huge billboard caught my eye. The image of a magnificent female, poised to gracefully execute her dive, was repeated six times. In each she modelled ideal form in a bathing suit of a different vivid colour. The only words were, "Daniel Hechter."

The promise implied in the media dimension was clear – simplicity, elegance, grace, a large colour selection, and a French shopping experience à la Daniel.

What did I experience in the physical dimension? A discount atmosphere with gondolas of clothing so tightly packed a flustered mother and her stroller couldn't even pass between them. The latest top ten tune blaring out of speakers at a decible level that, in a manufacturing environment, would surely have required safety ear plugs.

And the people dimension matched neither the media promise nor physical reality as teenage staff wearing very funky outfits bounced around the store in perfect time to the music. This group of employees could not have been more different from that which I was expecting if it had been planned. The result was complete disharmony.

I thought maybe I was in the wrong store, and double-checked the sign. How could I have been so gullible? How could I have wasted my time? But wait, maybe it wasn't my fault at all, maybe it was simply that "Daniel" had lied.

These are strong words representing even stronger emotions which no business would ever want to foster in a customer.

Even the most well-meaning effort to shoehorn a new concept into an existing business has the potential to replicate this disaster. What this company had done was to fail to understand the ways in which each dimension must exactly match the others. There was nothing wrong with the ad or physical store layout or the people, until those dimensions were measured against one another.

When a business rushes to incorporate great ideas that created "raving fans" for other service providers, they may unwittingly instead create disharmony as the new idea fails to match the existing reality. An advertising campaign that implies a "greeter at every door" to serve customers can't deliver that promise with a skeleton staff of unskilled part-timers.

PROMISE WHAT YOU DELIVER

It is a sad testimony of our times that the mantra in so many companies is "under promise and over deliver" as if the customer is some target to be duped. In fact, it doesn't matter what you promise just as long as you deliver it, consistently and that it is matched in all three dimensions of the business.

3-D harmony is a liberating concept for business. It saves time, energy, and money. Here is how one rather ordinary retailer built a fanatical loyal following, not by chasing every trend in a vain attempt to keep up with the Butterfly, but by taking a very simple concept and applying it consistently to every dimension of the business.

The Ugly Duckling—Honest Ed's

Back in the early '50s in Toronto, an entrepreneur created the city's first total discount department store. Since the building he bought was ugly to begin with, he decided to go all the way and painted the three-storey edifice in wild colours and silly slogans in letters big enough to read a block away. Inside, merchandise was thrown on roughly assembled wooden tables, stacked from planked floor to industrial ceiling, or hung on ugly metal racks. The few staff in evidence were so busy restocking merchandise that they ignored the customer entirely.

To attract customers, he created in-store events, some of which were probably done for the first time in a retail setting. Forties-style dance marathons brought customers who bebopped, jived, boogied, and shopped for two or three marathon days (and nights) amongst the aisles of clothing, housewares, and furniture. Every weekend, amazing opening specials attracted customers in droves and the Saturday morning line-up around the block awaiting the opening of Honest Ed's became a neighbourhood institution. The store was a phenomenal success. It was the first time the city had ever seen off duty police officers used for retail crowd control.

Since those days, many retailers have jumped on the discount bandwagon but none of them have had the nerve of Ed Mirvish. He has never succumbed to fancy renovations or slick, pretty advertising campaigns, or the call to service excellence. His cashiers are not the most pleasant of people and it is almost impossible to find help on the selling floor.

But crowds still gather on a Saturday morning and, over the years, Ed Mirvish has made enough profit to become a well-respected patron of the arts, revered by neighbours near and far. In a world filled with pretty stores whose windows are covered with "For Rent" signs, Honest Ed's has the beauty which matters—the loyalty of the Monarch Customer.

How can it be that a retail operation with so many "defects" earns customer loyalty while other seemingly "perfect" service providers have no guarantee of repeat business? Well, Honest Ed Mirvish succeeds in harnessing the power of the three dimensions by taking what is ordinary—a discount store—and make it extraordinary—a laughably, kitschy, ugly discount store—simply by ensuring every element is in harmony.

Preventing Disharmony

Keeping the dimensions in harmony also requires operational discipline. Let us tell you about an owner who was able to anticipate and prevent disharmony.

Domain was founded by the entrepreneurial and mercurial Judy George who, although cutting her retail teeth selling Scandinavian Modern, had a personal style that was far more romantic and whimsical. When she couldn't find a home furnishings store that met her personal requirements she opened her own furniture chain.

Like Honest Ed's, Domain is a model of three dimensions in harmony. Complete room settings featured in ads and brochures are replicated in the stores, down to the tiniest details. "Design expert" staff gladly show customers how to mix the "Tuscany" look with "Out of Africa."

One November, while working with Judy in her office, we were interrupted by the head of the advertising department who urgently required a decision on a print campaign scheduled for release the next day (a situation often occurring in the retail world). As Judy reviewed a very exciting, creative ad designed to increase Thanksgiving weekend traffic, she talked out her thoughts. "What will customers think when they see this? What will they expect to see in the stores? Do we have enough inventory in each store to replicate these room settings? What do the staff need in order to be able to be able to meet these expectations?"

As the conversation progressed, it became apparent that while the campaign was almost sure to increase traffic, there wasn't enough time for the store managers to stock their locations and train their staff with sufficient product knowledge. This is a common scenario in the busy world of retail and almost always, the decision is to "proceed because we can't afford to lose the opportunity for additional sales."

But that's not what Judy did. She rewarded the group for all their creativity, took responsibility for the lateness of the decision, and then cancelled the campaign. Her reasons for walking away from a forecasted 20% sales increase while having to bear the creative costs already incurred? Here is what she said to her advisory board.

> *"It was better to have reduced traffic than have customers attracted to a store that couldn't deliver the 'holistic' experience they have come to expect of us. If we're lucky, we can continue to fill those expectations for many years to come. The cost of turning off and disappointing some of those customers (whom we have already paid dearly to acquire) far outweighs any short term profit we could make from running the sale. It wouldn't be fair to our customers, our staff and in the long run, to our shareholders."*

Judy phoned all the stores, admitted she had screwed up, and that since they wouldn't have any new items or prices to feature, and maybe not much traffic either, they should concentrate on maximizing the opportunity with those customers who did come in.

Domain had one of its best holiday weekends ever in sales and gross margin. The result of deciding to halt was positive, yet the decision to "proceed as planned" is made daily in the service sector. The outcome? Great events—a sale, a product launch, a grand opening, etc.—may generate a short term increase in sales while contributing to diminishing trust as the execution fails to live in harmony with what the customer was promised. Yet another Butterfly Customer flits out of sight.

A New Measure of Business Success

The way business traditionally measures success (by reviewing sales results) makes it all too easy to miss the signals that warn you about the increasing percentage of your customers who are poised to flit off on the search for a more satisfying experience. Today's consumer is fickle, curious, and mobile. This Butterfly behaviour adds up to a deadly combination for those who insist on relying only on the traditional measures of sales, profits, and even repeat business.

Smart businesses bring a focus not only on the physical but on the *psychological* experience created for the customer. Following all the rules in the world won't help if visiting your business gives customers an Uh-oh feeling somewhere in the pit of their stomach.

The challenge of exorcising the disharmony from your organization is to learn how to identify and capture those moments that cause discomfort to your customers. You have to develop a tool that pinpoints when the dimensions are not in sync, and to isolate those moments when disharmony threatens to create a disenchanted customer.

Customers do record and measure the emotions and feelings you create for them as they experience your business. As owners and managers you had best learn to measure those customer responses. In the era of the Butterfly Customer, your survival is at stake.

CHAPTER FIVE

Measuring the Trust Account

S₀ HOW DOES a business measure trust? What will tell an executive or owner the degree of consistency between what is promised and what is delivered? How can disharmony and the incidence of Uh-oh feelings be quantified?

The process starts with understanding the concept of The Trust Account, that place where customers keep track of their level of trust in you. Understanding how the balance is built, and how to maintain it once it is built, provides the framework within which a company can set up its own audit system.

WHAT IS THE TRUST ACCOUNT?

The trust account is the sum total of a customer's experience with you. A positive balance in the trust account is the result of consistent delivery of the contract you have formed with your customer. And just as one incident of extraordinary service doesn't a loyal customer make, seldom does a single missed promise drive customers away forever, if there is any currency in the trust account at all. Let us look at two contrasting examples.

A Superhuman Feat and the Trust Account

In a sleepy town near a major resort area, a Korean woman opened a restaurant called the Wild Orchid. A group of friends from the big city decided to try it out, calling ahead to notify the owner and arrange a table.

As the group approached the strip plaza where the restaurant was located, their expectations ranged from none down to trepidation. But what the heck, they were just out for a good time and the company would provide that.

To their surprise, they were greeted at the door and led to a specially arranged set of tables where wine was quickly offered. The food was excellent, the presentation colourful, the staff attentive, and the owner on hand to introduce and explain as each new perfectly timed course arrived. It didn't matter that the wine was mediocre, the rest of the experience made up for it. Each member of the party vowed to return, to recommend it to others, and to bring a friend.

Some of the original gang actually did make the effort to trek the 20 miles based on that first outstanding visit. What they found this time was a restaurant experience as mediocre as the first visit's wine. The menu items weren't comparable to the owner-chosen dishes of that special night and the attentive service was nowhere in sight. Those who returned to the Wild Orchid soon warned the others, and the referrals, so desperately needed by a new restaurant, dried up.

The extra effort and expense required to create the superlative experience for the original group could never be affordably sustained during a regular night's business. Could this have been avoided? What could the owner have done to even out the service and gain more currency in her customer trust accounts?

If she had explained that for this size group she could afford to provide extra service and some special dishes, on the next visit expectations would have been more restrained. If she traded places with her wait staff from time to time throughout every evening, she could bring her personal interest to shine on every table, not just the one with the big party and big tab. Or if she let every customer know they could select from the special menu for a fee, she could provide unique dishes even for a table of two.

A Human Mistake and the Trust Account

Recently a colleague was in a Wal-Mart store in upstate New York. There was no greeter at the door and no staff in sight as she made her way to the music department. When she reached to serve herself with a Top-Ten Compact Disc, the entire display of 400 or so discs collapsed with a clatter. The words out of the mouth of the now-miraculously apparent sales associate were audible to the entire gathered crowd, "Whatever did you do?"

Is this incident enough to stop our colleague from going back to Wal-Mart? No. In fact she assumed it must have "just been an off day at the store." Something in her ten years spent observing, reading about, and experiencing this retailer had caused her to be forgiving of a behavioural lapse most consultants would have instantly added to their lore of appalling service stories. (You know, the ones which usually precede the myth about $6-an-hour stock clerks running down the highway to return a lost doll!) With a positive balance in the trust account, the odd human mistake will cause little or no harm. But when disaster does strike, companies who think in trust account terms are quick to take action to protect their trusting Monarch Customers.

PROTECTING THE TRUST ACCOUNT BALANCE

Certainly the response of Johnson and Johnson in 1989 when a pharmacy discovered some Tylenol bottles had been tampered with, is a perfect example of how to handle a potential deficit in the trust account. The company valued its credibility with the consumer more than the cost of recalling and repackaging the product. Within hours the entire shipment was off the shelf. Even though the company was clearly not responsible, not one corporate minute was wasted asking "Who was to blame?" Executives in this culture instinctively knew the answer to that question mattered not one iota to customers. The result? Hardly a ripple in corporate profits and a new standard for secure packaging appeared on everything from orange juice to tampons to lip balm. And, most importantly, Tylenol continued to enjoy the patronage of loyal customers during a time when many alternative products were becoming available.

By contrast, citing Exxon's behaviour after the drastic oil spill in Alaska one marketing consultant said, "Long after the slick has been washed from the bird feathers, Exxon will be remembered as a corporate bad guy."[1] The reason, he says, is that Exxon "never developed the kind of reputation that could have inoculated it against something like the Valdez spill." They had no credit in their customer trust account.

THE OPENING BALANCE SETS THE TONE

Understanding the opening balance in the trust account is essential to conducting an accurate assessment and creating an appropriate plan to fix it. Remember that collective memory we

---

[1] Kevin Clancy and Shulman Yankelovich Clancy: "The Payoff From a Good Reputation." *Fortune*, Feb. 10, 1992.

described in Chapter Two where entire industries such as auto, diet, and now even health care had created a consumer base of low trusters? Let us give you another example, within the context of the three dimensions and the trust account.

In the spring of 1996, Canadian TV viewers were assaulted by black and white ads featuring what looked like real people holding up signs that read: "ARE WE GOING TO BE OK?," "WILL I EVER OWN MY OWN HOME?," and "WHAT ABOUT US?" The overwhelming mood was that of the Great Depression.

Was this an ad for a charity? Was it a campaign to raise funds for the underprivileged? No, it was one of the slickest campaigns for a major Canadian bank we've ever seen.

Canada's Bank of Montreal wanted to position itself as a good corporate citizen. Entitled "Signs of the Times," the campaign, according to the creators at Vickers and Benson Advertising, "broke through" with the key 25 to 49 age group by publicly acknowledging the innermost feelings of disenchanted customers and delivering the key theme, "Can a bank change?" Or did they?

"CAN A BANK CHANGE?"

"HELL, WE DON'T EVEN MAKE CHANGE."

The always satirical *Frank* magazine may just have captured the instinctive response of most customers to the campaign in its April 1996 issue. So what if the target audience now knows through the media dimension that the bank understands how tough it is out there? Where is the proof in the physical and people dimensions that would demonstrate the bank is actually responding to all those plaintive signs written by customers?

Have service charges been lowered? Is a fledgling entrepreneur more likely to get an interest break, or a loan at all? Are teller lines shorter to ease the burden of modern family life? Do all those busy bees sitting at their desks, avoiding eye contact at all costs, finally look up, smile and come over to open another teller wicket?

During the very same fiscal period in which the ads were being aired, it was business as usual for the bank: record profits, just a little short of the billion dollar mark and up by almost 20% over the previous year; few if any perceived changes in the service performance of the branches we dealt with; 1,400 employees were laid off; and the chairman's compensation increased from $1.9 to $2.5 million.

Next time a voice-over on a television spot asks "Can A Bank Help?" we think the customers' response is going to be stronger than ever that banks only help themselves.

So, was this a bad campaign? No.

Was it a creative campaign? You bet!

But whether or not the customer comes to believe the bank *can* change rests solely in the harmony of this creative media message in the other two dimensions. It is unfortunate that the work wasn't done in the physical and people dimensions first so that the expectation created in the media could be matched in the experience.

The Bank of Montreal was on the right track. But the customer's collective memory and negative trust account balance will never be fixed by a one dimensional campaign. All three dimensions, working in perfect harmony are the only possible cure.

HOW DOES A COMPANY MEASURE ITS TRUST ACCOUNT?

To ascertain the balance in the trust account, a business must measure the gap between what is promised and what is delivered in every dimension of the business. Are we about to recommend another business audit: count this, tally that, map this process, chart it, graph it? Absolutely not. Forget the image of accountants hunkered down over reams of computer printouts. You don't need another unemotional, dispassionate look at the business. Instead imagine being a butterfly, flitting from place to place experiencing all the nuances of your business.

In order to take stock of the Butterfly Customer's response to your business, you have to feel what it is like to do business with you. It takes an emotional audit to get an emotional read on how customers *feel* as they wander through your business. Measuring the trust account requires a way to access the customer's subconscious expectations and subliminal experiences. What are they? How are they created? How closely do they match what you intended?

So just how do you find out how customers are feeling about the decision to do business with you? Do you attach them to electrodes to record their rising blood pressure as you deliver Uh-oh experiences? Will hypnosis reveal their subconscious feelings about your staff or product? What kind of audit or measurement system provides an accurate reading on something as intangible as trust?

The process must be simple and focus a company beyond the measure of how frequently customers return, to the measure of why they returned, what they did, and how they felt during the experience. What you have to do is to train your own inner voice to be heard. You have to learn to "see your business feelingly."

LEARN TO "SEE YOUR BUSINESS FEELINGLY"

"No eyes in your head...yet you see how this world goes,"
King Lear observes.
"I see things feelingly," the blinded Gloucester replies.

William Shakespeare, *King Lear,* Act IV, Scene 6.

In a way, you too need to be blind in order to see your business feelingly. You need to be blind to all the rationale, evidence, research, reasons, and excuses. Like Gloucester you need to move beyond the single dimension of sight to develop the ability to experience your business the way your customers do—in three dimensions.

It is true that life is much simpler when you look through a single lens. Read the sales numbers. Count the traffic. Record the coupon redemption. Examine the ad. Listen to the people. But human experience takes place in three dimensions. And if you don't learn the skill of seeing your business the way your customers experience it, you may unwittingly increase mistrust, even while trying to do something to please the customer.

See Like an Entrepreneur

Entrepreneurs start out with the instinct to see the business feelingly because in the beginning they are their own customers. They identify a personal need or want and develop a product or service to meet that need. The design of the store or the business reflects their personal likes, dislikes, and tastes. Since they know the most about the product and the presentation, they can talk to the customer about its design and use in terms filled with passion and intelligence. They are all three dimensions of the business rolled up in one human being.

Warren Rubin—Long Live the Customer

A great example of an entrepreneur who feels his business is Warren Rubin, founder and chairman of the Workbench furniture chain. For more than 35 years, Warren and Workbench have been designing and selling furniture that meets the needs of a certain customer, and that customer is Warren, whose own home is the perfect showcase for his product. It is his values that drive every product design. "I don't care if the customer doesn't see that the line on the Shaker piece is absolutely true to the original design, I see it." Since Warren is interested in how furniture is made, his customers have been receiving product knowledge from the store staff, brochures, and newsletters since day one. And, it's no surprise to learn that the company has been conducting weekly product knowledge training for staff for years.

Warren is the merchant, the customer, and the marketer. It is his view that is reflected in every dimension of the business. No wonder it's seamless and in harmony. Warren's customers, although exhibiting Butterfly behaviour in almost all aspects of their lives, are Monarchs when it comes to his store because he has been loyal to his values. The Breuyer chair they purchased and loved 35 years ago is still available in every one of the 40 stores today because Warren wants furniture that lasts a lifetime. Is this a very expensive product to last so long? Not at all. Workbench found a way to deliver Warren's standards of high quality with moderate prices.

Maybe you think that this harmony is easier in a two or four or even 40 location chain than it is in a megacorporation. Easier maybe, but it is possible at any size.

Sam Walton

No matter how large his company became, he always had the instinct which let him see his business feelingly. What is natural and easy for the entrepreneur who lives the business in the shoes of the customer every day was replicated by Walton in millions of square feet separated by thousands of miles.

There are millions of opportunities to get things wrong, and certainly there are occasional misses in the service experience at Wal-Mart. But overall, Sam built a high degree of trust with customers by ensuring a company in harmony.

In the legion of Sam stories, many of which have taken on the status of urban legend, our favourites are those about how he toured his stores and listened to customers and associates. According to one former Wal-Mart vice-president, Sam's shirt-sleeve style meant he fit right into the landscape as he trolled the aisles looking for ideas about how to improve the business. Certainly many customers never knew they were part of this billion-dollar company's customer research as they responded to simple, direct questions about their shopping experience. Sam asked their opinions, heard their stories about doing business with Wal-Mart, and paid attention to what they said.

Even in the gigantic Wal-Mart of his later years he never lost his entrepreneurial instinct to get into the field. Perhaps he arrived by corporate jet instead of by pick-up truck, but the purpose of a visit was always the same—to actively seek out the feeling of the business from the best vantage point, standing in the shoes of and seeing through the eyes of the customer and the employee.

T I P

OBJECTIVE: To feel what customers feel as they experience your product.

PROCESS: Set aside what you know about the business and pretend you are a customer during a visit. Don't start with the back rooms, in fact don't even go there. Just pick up an ad and decide what it leads you to expect, walk up to the premises or dial up the number, and experience the service.

TACTIC: Try to be as anonymous as possible. Visit a remote location, wear casual clothes, and never reveal your identity. It is amazing how different that experience can feel from a formal visit.

Warren Rubin and Sam Walton are just two of many entrepreneurs who have used the filter of their own inner voices to test which ideas and suggestions fit with the natural order they have created, and discard the ones that would take their concept out of harmony. They have a gut instinct about how to see their business feelingly.

The concept of replicating this ability of the entrepreneur to feel the perspective of the customer has been called by many different names. Whether it's "walk the talk" as Carole Cox of Frank's Nursery in Detroit and a veteran human resources vice-president describes it, or the hot flash consulting phrase "management by walking around," the activity should be the same: replicate the ability of the small entrepreneur to deliver three dimensions in harmony because they feel the experience just as the customer does.

THE 3-D AUDIT

A 3-D Audit is the process tool we use to measure the gap between the expectations and the delivery, through the eyes, heart, and mind of each of your customers. The magnitude of that gap is what determines the level of trust and loyalty. It decides whether your customers are Butterflies or Monarchs.

Your customers instinctively do something similar to this audit every time they experience your business, so do you when you are someone else's customer. You need to call upon this inherent emotional audit skill and learn to apply it to your own business. Like Gloucester in *King Lear*, Warren Rubin at Workbench, and the late Sam Walton, you need to see your business feelingly.

A 3-D Audit simply reminds everyone in the business of how to feel the experience and recognize those notes of disharmony which eat away at trust. It forces you and your team to set aside what you know and focus instead on the emotional impact you are delivering the customer as they experience you in three dimensions.

There are three major parts to a 3-D Audit. They are:

1. The Expectations Contract
2. 3-D Integration Breeds Harmony
3. Organization and Culture

The Expectations Contract

The objective of this aspect is to examine your contract with your customers. If you are looking at your business through the eyes of your customer, you must begin by ensuring you understand exactly what those customers believe you promised them. It is not what *you think* you are saying to your customers, but what *they hear*.

The Expectations Contract is a fluctuating set of promises over which you have frighteningly little control. On the one hand, you can determine your proper place in the market place and your "unique selling proposition." It is here where you have the greatest influence setting customer expectations, by deciding exactly what you are all about and how you want to position yourself in the market place in terms of the economy and the competition.

On the other hand, customers live in a complex world over which you have no control, and everything they read, hear, or see affects their expectations of you. That is why this first section of a 3-D Audit includes a discussion on the moods of the customer. No audit is complete without a look at the potential influences both inside and outside the organization and an analysis of how they are affecting customer expectations.

3-D Integration Breeds Harmony

The match between customer expectations and how a business adjusts its delivery of the 3-D kaleidoscope defines the level of trust enjoyed with customers. Understanding the degree of harmony in the overall experience requires a detailed look at each of the three dimensions.

In the **Media Dimension**, you must review all the planned and unplanned messages which customers are receiving about your business and ensure you understand the implications of those messages on the delivery in the other two dimensions.

Because the **Physical Dimension** is often a fixed asset consuming vast amounts of capital, present and planned investments must be designed so they work in tandem with the other two dimensions.

The **People Dimension** is the one over which you have the least control. You can courier camera-ready ad materials, send the construction codes, or modem product specifications with confidence that the end result will match the original design. But when it comes to people, your vision will be interpreted by individuals. It is no wonder that this dimension is the one where we often see those subtle misses that eat away at trust. This dimension deserves your greatest attention, if disharmony is to be avoided.

Organization and Culture

And finally, a 3-D Audit must look at Organization and Culture. Because it is not just what you do, but how you do it, that garners the trust which creates Monarch Customers. Only a walk through the interior of your business will help you truly understand your ability to deliver a customer experience free from discord.

If you believe trust is the critical measure for long-term success in the service sector, you had better audit your trust account with your customers constantly. That is the measure that will tell you what your customer's subconscious is muttering, regardless of whether or not they spent money with you today.

This audit isn't easy but is a critical step in determining how you are doing. In consulting with our clients, once we have established just what the customer contract should be, we advise them to validate every action against the question "How does this help or hinder us in delivering our customer contract and developing a trusting environment?" The following chapters describe the process we use in enough detail to allow you to take a hard look at your own business, beginning with How to Conduct a 3-D Audit.

Conducting a 3-D Audit

THE CLIENT CALL for help came in terms of a desire for a specific solution. "We need a training program for our front-line staff to improve our service levels," said Jim Null, newly appointed director of operations for Berean Christian Bookstores, an eighteen-store chain with annual sales of $50 million.

Having been in this retail sector for nearly twenty years, he knew of us through a training productivity system that had worked for a previous employer and wanted the same magic for his new team.

Before agreeing upon the solution we want to know the who, what, when, where, why, and how of the position a company finds itself in. And so instead of receiving the panacea of an instant fix, this U.S. retailer's simple request was met with a series of probing questions:

- What is it you think an investment in training will do for you?
- What are the results from your existing training programs?
- What would the front-line people tell us about their current service levels?

- How do your customers rate your current levels of service?
- What extra profit do you expect an increase in service levels to bring your shareholders?

By the third or fourth question Jim began feeling uncomfortable and admitted, "As much as I want to believe that a few simple steps would fix everything, I know by the questions I can't answer that maybe rushing to institute a training program is the wrong approach—at least until we know ourselves better."

THE 3-D AUDIT OBJECTIVE

Perhaps the best outcome of a 3-D Audit is to know thyself more intimately. To see oneself through the eyes of the customer. To be able to feel the business the way customers and staff do. This degree of self-awareness provides much of the information required to know how to turn the ever increasing numbers of Butterfly Customers into loyal Monarchs.

It takes nerves of steel to agree to undergo such intense scrutiny. After all, customers are ones' harshest critics. So why would a financially successful, growing company expose itself to the gaze of "fresh eyes" that see everything and are, in fact, paid to bring forward unpleasant truths? Dan Miles, Berean's vice-president and general manager shares his reasons:

> *"I knew we couldn't sustain the pattern set by fourteen straight quarters of growth in sales and profits from our existing operation and so would be challenged to open new stores in new markets. But I was already consumed managing the stores we had. How would we continue to meet the expectations of shareholders for profits and growth while maintaining the integrity of the operation for customers and staff? When Jim suggested that before we invest in a training*

program we get a better understanding of our business, I was prepared to listen."

And so Berean embarked on a journey of self-discovery through experiencing the 3-D Audit. Before we discuss each step in detail and how Berean fared in the process, here are the six steps:

STEP ONE: Engage the Team
STEP TWO: Feast on the Facts
STEP THREE: Feel the Experience
STEP FOUR: Gauge the Gaps
STEP FIVE: Describe the Harmony
STEP SIX: Engage the Team…Again

STEP ONE: ENGAGE THE TEAM

The objective in this step is to ensure the staff are ready and able to contribute to an intense look at the business. Just telling them about the audit isn't enough. Although each company must deal with its own unique situation, examining what Dan did and why can be helpful in setting out your own plan to engage your team.

He Picked the Right Time

Even though he believed in the value of an external look at the business, Dan wisely chose to wait nearly eighteen months before starting the formal audit. With a long-awaited computer implementation just underway, he instinctively felt the stress the organization would be under. He knew it would be very difficult to engage the team while they were being consumed with tough operational issues. Waiting for the audit was better than losing effectiveness because the team didn't have the time or energy needed to participate fully and be committed to the outcome.

In your own organization, before embarking on an audit make sure you are starting at the right time. Ask yourself: are we heavily engaged, or about to be, in a new activity or process? Have we recently changed our product mix, operating style, or ownership? Are we under enormous competitive or market place pressure? If the answer to these questions is yes, in addition to staff being "too busy" to contribute at this time, there is also the risk of what we call observation contamination. This happens when a special circumstance ends up being the cause of every effect. For instance, at Berean, Dan and Jim knew that the installation of the new computer had begun to be the "reason" (at least in the eyes of the employees) for everything from long customer line-ups, to an increase in staff resignations, and the expensive payroll overages.

His Team Helped Design the Project

Dan knew his own people well enough to empathize with the tension engendered by the prospect of a "service audit." During the time leading up to formal start of the audit, he did several things to increase comfort levels and, ultimately, project effectiveness.

First, he used several managers' meetings to introduce the concept of the three dimensions and the plan to audit the organization. He invited the consultants into the sessions to allow the managers an opportunity to get comfortable with the players and explore the concepts. Through these activities, he increased the likelihood of active participation by his managers in the process.

Second, a small committee of well-respected managers helped to fine-tune the actual contract terms and confirm the selection of the contractor. Finally, the operating committee was given an overview of the project prior to the start date.

He Gave Permission To Speak Freely

How a company communicates the 3-D Audit to the balance of the organization has a direct impact on the quality of the information gathered, and how quickly the auditor can move beyond platitudes to the heart of the matter. Too many head offices set an organizational review in motion without fully disclosing the reasons behind management's quest for change and how it might affect its employees. There is nothing more unsettling to staff than hearing that some "consultant" is nosing around!

Unlike a sneak attack by tax auditors, a 3-D Audit wants the participants to have as much warning as possible. The resultant quality of information and insights is greatly improved when the team has time to prepare and is given "permission" to speak freely.

At Berean that happened because of several things. First, the team was informed by letter and in team meetings about why the service audit was being undertaken. Second, people were assured of confidentiality and told about the research methods that would guarantee comments or ideas could not be attributed to individuals unless they requested it. Finally, the team was given an overview of the process and the different ways in which they could contribute. This included a timetable of expected events such as store visits and company-wide surveys. Through these actions Dan created a team ready and willing to participate in an important, organizational effort.

OBJECTIVE: To ensure maximum input from the team by involving individuals and giving them permission to speak freely.

PROCESS: Provide key leaders/managers with the big picture about what a 3-D Audit is designed to do and why you feel the time is right to conduct one. If you are using a consultant to help (which is generally recommended), explain why an outside view is useful.

Focus on what a 3-D Audit does for *all* the stakeholders in the business. Be especially careful to communicate the benefits for customers and employees.

Provide very specific details about how the information will be gathered and what you are doing to protect confidentiality. Cite the credentials of any outside consultant or explain the steps the internal team will take to protect their sources, such as a pre-stamped envelope so the origin of the survey won't be known, or an electronic format which removes the need for recognizable handwriting.

Eliminate surprises by making it clear what employees can expect to be asked to do or contribute. For instance, if there will be a company-wide survey, say so.

Make a promise about when and how the results will be reported back to employees. And, if you find you can't keep that promise, let the team know in advance.

TACTIC: Give "ownership" to departments and units through the use of small group meetings. Provide the leaders/managers with a script which includes both the facts and the answers to frequently-asked questions such as "Will we be paid for attending off-site interviews?"

He Involved Those Who Pay the Bills

An audit has a price tag. If there is an external consultant there are fees. But even during an internal audit the team may incur travel and research costs. Regardless of who creates the research questions, conducts the interviews, analyses the data, and writes the report, there is the time of everyone involved in gathering information and answering questions.

Someone is paying those bills and they must see the potential value of the investment. Berean did a cost-benefit analysis and spoke to other business leaders who had received concrete business results through similar processes. Armed with concrete examples and estimates of the costs, Dan could comfortably assure those who represent the owners/stockholders that this was an investment that had been validated against the financial imperatives of the business.

Dan and the engaged team were now ready for step two of the audit process. The timing was right. Team leaders had been given time to get used to the concept and to gain comfort with the consultant. The field had been given permission to speak. The executive understood the reason for the investment. And everyone was waiting to see what would happen next.

STEP TWO: FEAST ON THE FACTS

"This is a very long list." Jim Null's voice reached across the long-distance line, begging to understand why we would be requesting enough current data and history to fill three large boxes at the outset of a project to plan the future of the company.

The request had been for over twenty items ranging from job descriptions, sample ads, store signs, brochures, computer printouts, internal audit forms, a sample employee personnel file, inventory records, to financial statements. Jim was right to be curious about our desire to wallow in all sorts of facts.

Here is the objective of this step in the 3-D Audit process. There is no better way to plan for the future than to begin by becoming immersed in the present. Since the essence of who you are is evident in every document, every policy, every memo, and every communication with customer or employee, an auditor must experience the full range. Here is what we do to ensure we truly feel your company the way all your customers do.

Decide What Questions You Want Answered

There are a myriad of questions which are answered by feasting on the facts of the business. What are the staff being told about the upcoming promotional piece that is going out to the customer? How is "success" measured and reported to staff, management, and shareholder or owner? How many different people touch each decision to undertake a store renovation, sign a new lease, commit to a billboard, or give an employee a raise? Are the same issues such as theft, or errors in documentation discussed over and over? How many times are duplicate messages, conflicting messages, and/or "corrections" to previous memos sent? Do the messages accurately reflect the stated philosophy of the company?

Locate the Source Documents

To know what information is required to assess your business, think about all the places where you might look for the answer to these types of questions. And, include everything you communicate to your front-line managers and staff. We always ask to receive all ongoing mail (fax, phone messages, e-mail, memos) that a typical site would receive in a typical week or two. Time and again clients are at first astounded and then dismayed when we arrive at their offices carting reams of paper or hundreds of e-mail messages which represent a mere week or two of internal memos.

TIP

> **OBJECTIVE:** To ensure the auditors have a complete picture of the present situation.
>
> **PROCESS**: Set up the audit office to replicate a front-line operation or remote location. Include a copy of every policy, job description, memo, and training manual available.
>
> **TACTIC:** Create a "dummy" operation (branch, department, or store) which will receive every internal communication going out to the field from every internal department.

Review the Pile of Paper With Fresh Eyes

What happens to the information once gathered? Within two weeks of putting the request to Jim, large boxes began arriving at our office where consultants, (highlighters and Post-it notes in hand) descended upon the mass of communication. From what was there, and what was not there, we began to form a picture of the business.

As the paper piled higher and higher over the next few weeks, we feasted (and subsequently choked) on facts in preparation for the next stage of the audit. We were now ready to throw away the slide rule, turn off the computer, put away the calculator, and willingly walk through the looking glass into a world of curiosity and confusion where we could feel the experience of shopping at Berean, working at Berean, managing Berean, and owning Berean.

STEP THREE: FEEL THE EXPERIENCE

The objective of this step is to ensure what we are hearing and feeling is in harmony. If something creates a shadow it's time to take a closer look. When something causes that Uh-oh feeling we dig around to find out what it is. If a customer grins while a shareholder grimaces, we insist on knowing why.

And that last comment is why, before describing how this next step is accomplished, we first have to describe the overall perspective we take. The 3-D Audit is not customer-centric. The customer is just one of the players who must experience a harmonious, Uh-oh-free world. The employee and the shareholder are the two other, equally important, stakeholders.

Three Perspectives

Here is the perspective of each of the three stakeholders and some of the techniques used to uncover the feelings of each.

The Shareholder/Owner

Keeping the view of the shareholder requires close attention to traditional measures of business success. You must be able to consider any findings in light of their potential effect on quarter-by-quarter operating results, return on invested capital, net profit, etc. But what about emotions? How can one "feel" the experience of being an investor in a business?

Sometimes it is easy. Many of our clients are entrepreneurs who are the owner/shareholder of the business as well as the key manager. In addition to the typical factors such as inventory levels which the bank might value, more personal yardsticks are easy to find. For instance, one of our clients was building a business for the next generation. In his 3-D Audit, we needed to feel what business decisions were being made because he wanted to create a family legacy. Sacrificing short-term gains for long-term success was a strategy he was following.

We gather these perspectives by undertaking a series of activities with the owner or manager. We take time to linger over coffee and discuss general business issues. We jointly check out the competition and visit key locations together. We ask probing questions about their desires for the business in the short and long term.

Even in mega-corporations there can be a personal element to the shareholder perspective. At Berean, the then-president was nearing retirement and wanted to leave his successor a strong financial base on which to support future growth. Understanding this objective explained a great deal about how the business was being run in the field, for instance, the emphasis on the fundamental discipline of managing the numbers.

The Employee

Employees have valuable information to share about what it is like to be in the middle between the customer and the shareholder. We consider facts such as who is hired or promoted, how long they stay, how people are paid, and what their job description says they should do compared to what they really do. But we also want to know how individuals are making the decisions about what they do during a day, how they deal with conflicting demands from other stakeholders, and what pleases them most, and least, about coming into work each day. We want to see the customer and the company through the eyes of the employee. How much do they know about the consumer and the competition and how accurate are their impressions of the job they do compared to those of their bosses?

We use several techniques to gather this information. The first is a variety of surveys relating to attitude, perceptions of skill levels, and operational issues. Another is that of the individual or group interview. This more "open-ended" approach gets staff discussing how they feel about issues and procedures.

OBJECTIVE: Experience what your employees really feel and believe about the business, not just what they think you want to hear.

PROCESS: Survey the morale, hold one-on-one and group interviews and conduct 360-degree surveys to uncover the gaps between perception and reality. A 360-degree audit is a process where the behaviour of one group is assessed in three ways: self-assessment, assessment of those for whom the individual works (the boss), and assessment by those the individual supports or serves (employees and customers).

TACTIC: Go and get HELP!

This is one area where we emphatically will not endorse the do-it-yourself approach. Poorly designed questions or badly managed interviews will cost you something far greater than the dollars you spend on this endeavour. If you select an outside source experienced in your industry, the added benefit is that it allows you to benchmark your results against other similar industries, or even direct competitors.

Finally, in addition to surveys and individual or group interviews, it is important to stand directly in the shoes of the employee. Job-shadowing, following the staff as they go about their daily routines, helps put policies and procedures in perspective.

The Customer

Getting at what customers feel is critical. What are they expecting as they approach the business? What are they feeling as they conduct their transaction and walk out the door? How does this compare to their feelings about other businesses they like, and dislike? What behaviours do these feelings generate?

The problem with relying on most traditional customer research techniques to provide these insights is that they are only cerebral. Even though the question asked is "How does this make you feel?" the response is cognitive. The question and answer has to be interpreted through a thinking process which can cloak the intensity of the emotions. When the customer experiences Uh-oh feelings on levels so deep that even they are hard-pressed to articulate what is making them uncomfortable, traditional research techniques often can't uncover the subtle misses between expectation and experience. In Chapter Eight we will provide you with insights on how to adapt the traditional research techniques of focus groups and behavioural observations to get at what and how consumers are feeling about a business.

So now that we have explored the perspectives we want to take, let us present the two actions which accomplish the objective of this step.

Ask Everyone the Same Question

Every stakeholder should be asked exactly the same set of questions, but from their own perspective. Get employees to tell you how they are managed. Ask their managers how they manage the employees. Ask customers what happens when they have a problem requiring management intervention and their perceptions of how the company is managed. Gather customers' ratings of the skills of the staff with whom they interact. Then, ask those staff to rate their own service skills, and their managers to evaluate the performance of these same staff. Ask accounting about the kinds of communication they have with the field, and the front line about the financial requests which come from head office. Ask customers to describe how different processes affect their experience.

Ask Every Question More Than One Way

Never use just a single research methodology. Interview customers, but also conduct group interviews with staff to discuss results. Use behavioural observations to follow customer and staff interactions and surveys to record responses. Get responses to the same questions in more ways than one to give you an added perspective and to validate what you think you saw.

Throughout the audit we constantly keep our antenna high in anticipation of the gaps in all three dimensions. By constantly looking at an issue from multiple points of view, asking everyone the same questions, and asking questions more than one way, we are able to see the, sometimes gaping, holes between perceptions or expectations and the reality of the experience.

STEP FOUR: GAUGE THE GAPS

In this step the objective is to take the three perspectives of the key stakeholders and integrate them. Remember the entrepreneurs who could instinctively prevent disharmony because they are the customer, the employee, and the shareholder? That is exactly who we imitate in this step.

There is really only one technique we use and that is to take every piece of information we have on a key issue and plot it against all the other information we have. For instance, when it comes to perceptions of service, we would compare what customers said about what service they wanted, versus how they behaved in the store. We would then combine that with what we had seen employees do during our visits with how managers evaluated their skill. And we would add to the analysis the job descriptions, the interview tapes, the payroll records, and so on. We copy the entrepreneur and all three stakeholders combined into one.

And so in gauging the gaps, we find differences in expectations, perceptions, and experiences. Some are minor and easily fixed. Others are multidisciplinary and may require a retooling of procedures or practices. One note. Rather than seeing the gaps as a failing of the organization, we present them as opportunities to improve. You don't have to be sick to get better!

Knowing the gaps is not enough. A framework for future decisions must be provided. Which gaps are going to provide the greatest good when closed? Which gaps are worth the effort and expenditure? In order to facilitate these decisions, a 3-D Audit should describe the vision of the world in which trust is a matter of course, where customers are Monarchs while staff and shareholders bask in the positive effects. And that leads us to Step Five in the process.

STEP FIVE: DESCRIBE THE HARMONY

Having listened to all three stakeholders and having spent time in every dimension of the business, we have a strong notion of what is expected and what can be delivered. It is up to the client to determine what to do with the information. The objective of this step is to communicate what we have seen in clear language, with plenty of examples and facts, and a certain degree of fearlessness. Why do we need to be fearless? Because we may challenge fundamental beliefs or provide a contrarian viewpoint. And we never, ever stop asking uncomfortable questions such as "Why are you doing this?" Every executive who has engaged in this process will tell you that "getting the report" is the toughest part of all.

Select the Appropriate Medium

A 3-D Audit has value only if those affected believe the findings and how we deliver the message often has as much influence as what is said. What is the "right" presentation style? The answer is dictated by the organization. Some prefer a set of graphs or overheads which capture key points. Others want a full report with many appendices. Most often we provide an Executive Overview, followed by a written report, followed up by personal presentations of the information where we hope to get back as much probing curiosity as we exhibited during the process.

Double-Check the Facts

This is the time when it is critical to ensure the facts are correct and the conclusions make sense. We often use a small internal group to test the findings, facts, details, and language. Since we are talking about important issues and our goal is to convince the audience of the accuracy of the findings, we wouldn't want to lose a reader or listener over an inaccurate fact or incomplete detail.

Create a Story for the Audience

We have found the best way to present the results is to tell the story in a structured way. Beginning with a summary of key findings (for those Butterflies in the audience who just want to skim through the surface), we follow on with a compelling look at the world outside their business. Often executives find this the most interesting aspect of the report as they lift their heads from the daily routine and become immersed in the world of their customers. They realize how much important information they haven't seen because they were on the busy-work treadmill instead of being out with the customer. Then we guide the reader onto the emotional roller coaster of the three dimensions. We want the team to soar with delight in those moments of glorious harmony and experience the chill of the shadow.

And we conclude where our audience is most likely to be uncomfortable, with the gaps in their own management styles or practices. While it may have been fun to laugh at the stories about what goes on in the back room of a store, it is not quite so amusing to hear what the staff said about how they are treated by management. As one client said to us, *"It's like taking a bad tasting medicine but you gotta do it in order to get better."*

After the 3-D Audit report is completed and presented to key management, we are ready for the final step:

Engage the Team...Again.

STEP SIX: ENGAGE THE TEAM...AGAIN

And so, we come full circle. All the credibility we earned throughout the process can be lost due to poor follow-up. All the insights gained are worth nothing if they are not acted upon. Equally important to the audit start is the audit finish and a report to the executive is not the finish. We need to go back to all of those we engaged in Step One, complete the communication loop and bring closure to this phase of the process. We seldom leave this step entirely in the hands of our clients. While some of the messages may be tough, the audit should never attack individuals. It takes a skilled facilitator to protect self-esteem and maintain a positive mood throughout this roller-coaster ride.

Key Team Members, First

In the case of Berean, you'll remember that Dan formed a small committee of seasoned managers and involved the Operating

Committee and store managers. In an off site, four day meeting, each key participant was provided with a personal copy of the report so they could read and absorb it before having to discuss it. We made sure that they had sufficient time to talk about any findings that affected them personally and discuss the implications with the report's authors.

After a vigorous discussion, the group was ready to come up with a strategy for determining which gaps to address and in which order. They then worked together to deliver suggestions for goals and tactics to achieve the objective of closing the gaps and delivering an experience that would meet the needs of all three stakeholders. Some very creative initiatives came out of this workshop and gave Dan and the executive a list of options that could be implemented quickly.

The Same Information To Everyone

In order to avoid the situation where some (favoured) employees seem to get better information than others, before leaving, the team prepared and practiced a presentation they would make to their staff and each made a commitment that by a certain date, every employee in the company would have received exactly the same feedback in exactly the same way, thereby closing the communication loop with the employees and demonstrating the commitment to anonymity.

In Step Six, the company met the promise made in Step One: to provide feedback in a certain way, by a certain date.

BEREAN THEN AND NOW

So let us summarize the Berean experience of the 3-D Audit.

Since the early '90s, Berean Christian Bookstores, a retailer of religious and spiritual information, entertainment, and gifts, has been undergoing extensive changes as it repositioned itself for growth. A key issue in this business, as it is for many retailers, was how to pare down inventory levels. The answer was a sophisticated computer system that linked buyers to store sales information. One of the first major changes the company initiated was the purchase and installation of a new point-of-sale system designed to pare down inventory costs. Within two-and-half years of that installation, ROI (Return On Investment) had soared to 27%. The stockholders were very happy! However, Berean executives, by their own admission, admit it was blind faith that kept the retailer going through those years of working through the new system's glitches. Sales associates were in a heads-down mode at computer terminals while customers and head office requests were being ignored.

During this systems period, head office, so focused on its beyond-forecasted return to the stockholder, had forgotten about the customer and the employee. They had forgotten to take into account the burden on store employees of running parallel systems for a test year. They had forgotten to write new responsibilities and details into job descriptions. And, they had forgotten that something had to give in order for the employees to deliver what was being asked. That something was customer service.

When Service Dimensions was invited onto the scene, the company's ROI had been ratcheted to extremely high levels through managing by numbers. However, the company's human ledger had dipped into a deficit. Controlling costs and numbers had a positive effect on profit and showed significant growth but we know that in order for real growth to be sustained, it has to be driven from both sides of the ledger.

Today at Berean, all three dimensions are in sync. An intensive focus on giving the employees the tools and training has paid off in the levels of customer service provided. How do we know? Because sales are up, mystery customer evaluations are improving, and every member of the team can translate the strategy into personal performance objectives.

FROM THE SPECIFIC TO THE GENERAL

Every company is unique. What we found at Berean and the exact way in which things happened, will never be replicated in any other operation.

But in the process of doing 3-D Audits for retail, hospitality and tourism, utilities, service providers, and manufacturers, several strong themes arose. These are the gaps which occur across the sectors and which greatly affect the ability of a Butterfly to ever gain the comfort which leads to trust and to Monarch behaviour. These are:

No Strategy, where companies do not have a single goal and a plan to get there, causing them to be subject to every new whim or idea which comes along. Being customer-responsive does not require an organization to be without its own point of view.

The Expectations Contract: Misreading the Customer, in which corporations lose their way to the customers heart by misreading expectations or losing touch with the mood of the customer and what's going on in their world.

The Media Dimension: Attractive Offer or Fatal Attraction?, in which we explore how companies do such a great job selling the story in the media dimension that customers may be disappointed in the reality.

The Physical Dimension: The Emperor's New Clothes, in which the company gets so caught up in its external coverings they don't realize that these expensive trappings are of little or no value to the Butterfly Customer.

The People Dimension: No Value Added, where we explore how companies fail to deliver the promise of the first two dimensions in the one that counts the most.

Internal Affairs: *Culture Clash,* where you can learn how organization and management may negatively affect the number of Monarch Customers you attract.

These gaps are the subject of the next six chapters. And, as was the case here, owing to the generosity of our clients in allowing us to tell their stories, you can experience first-hand some of the problems and the solutions.

No Strategy

A HIGHWAY WITH no end. A voyage with no map. If you don't know where you are going, any road will get you there. These phrases describe the aimless activities of all too many retail and service companies on their endless chase to catch up to the Butterfly Customer.

Oh sure. They have the words all right: vision, mission, values, strategy, goals, objectives, plans. But the buzz words of modern corporate life create only noise as they remain a series of things to do instead of an integrated link on the chain. It is the word strategy, the word in the middle, that joins together the core reasons a business exists with the practical realities of running it professionally.

The gap of *no strategy* happens when a business has no way to marry its vision of who it is and what is about with an operating plan of action that ensures both consistency with the vision and a responsiveness to the demands of the market place.

WHAT IS STRATEGY?

Strategy is not just planning. According to Peter Drucker, "*Planning* tries to optimize tomorrow, the trends of today. *Strategy* aims to exploit the new and different opportunities of tomorrow."[1]

In terms of the Butterfly Customer, having a strategy means that the company has devoted sufficient time to understand what might happen to their business if the customers stop doing X and start doing Y. Strategy earns you an even chance at being able to keep your business in tune with the ever changing Butterfly Customer.

WHAT IS YOUR STRATEGY?

The following has occurred more than once during a 3-D Audit. Whether the company is an international manufacturer, a major utility, or a privately-held specialty retailer, it is amazing the number of times we ask:

> "*Describe your strategy to leverage your position in the marketplace.*"

only to get the following response...

> "............................."

That's right. Dead air. No answer, even when we ask the question in a number of different ways. Those we are interviewing lack a strategy to execute the vision, mission, and values of the business. Why is this? Why do so many companies neglect this critical piece? We think it is because traditional strategic planning models no longer work.

---

[1] Peter Drucker, *Managing in Turbulent Times* (New York: Harper & Rowe, 1980), pp. 60, 61.

The Tortoise and the Hare

Once upon a time, the process that led to strategy emulated the behaviour of the tortoise in the children's story of his race with the hare. The hare, so confident of her speed, veered off the course to investigate new things and, ultimately, to take a nap. Meanwhile, the slow, methodical tortoise, following his plan to the letter, passed the sleeping hare to reach the finish line first. Being focused on a single goal (the finish line) and faithful to his plan (a straight line) won the day. By the 1980s, it was the hare's behaviour that represented the ideal. Fast and flexible became the bywords of corporate success. Quick response, rapid change in direction, and instant abandonment of established plans in favour of new ones identified this era. For these companies, "strategic planning" was considered an outmoded notion that was replaced by "continuous improvement" and a constant, evolving target.

Today neither approach works. The tortoise-like company suffers paralysis by analysis—any proposed deviation from the straight and narrow requires altogether too much decision-making time and effort. And the hares? They are busy jumping on the latest bandwagon, trying to shoehorn the latest customer service initiative into their operation, and reacting to every change in consumer behaviour with a new tactic. Their rampant desire to run off in all directions may interest Butterflies on the lookout for something new, but rewards no one else.

So how does an organization create a strategy which will deliver the corporate mission in an operating environment over which they have ever diminishing control? Although there are no certainties in today's business world, the profiles of companies where strategy has enabled the values of the company to be effectively delivered within the ever changing operating realities of the Butterfly era exemplify what we call The Four F Behaviour: focused, faithful, flexible, and fast.

THE FOUR F BEHAVIOUR

Focused centres everyone on a core vision, mission, and values through creating a unique selling proposition and ensuring that everyone understands the implications for how the business is run.

Faithful requires a system to measure and evaluate the fidelity —not to the structured plan, but to the selling proposition and core values.

Flexible is the recognition that there is always more than one "right" way to get from here to there and that this new breed of customer is not only always changing needs but creating new ones that require an adaptation of the original design.

Fast is having the crisp operations and processes required to execute change in a nanosecond to ward off an impending competitive threat, handle an unforeseen situation, or take advantage of an opportunity.

FOCUS: CREATE COMMON GROUND

The company that has written its vision from the heart and defined a unique selling proposition is a company that has taken the first critical step in building trust with the Butterfly Customer. This company has clearly laid out in its own mind what it wants the customer to expect and receive from any interaction. It can confidently move to create three dimensions which are aligned with that strategy.

What Is a Unique Selling Proposition?

The phrase "a unique selling proposition" dates from 1953 when it was coined by Doyle, Dane Bernbach Advertising. It is, quite simply, the sum total of what you promise the customer. In the old model, it was created in the executive suite and communicated through the creative endeavours of the advertising and marketing departments. The new model involves the front line (those charged with delivering it) in the design to ensure the skills required to be successful are in place.

It is not just what you say in the media dimension about your product or service, but also about what you do in the physical and people dimensions that communicates your proposition to the customer. It is the reason customers should choose to deal with you and describes how you are different from your competitors. Slogans such as MacDonalds, "You deserve a break today," Ford's "Quality is Job One," and Eaton's old "Satisfaction Guaranteed" are all communicating the selling proposition the company is offering the customer. If done correctly in all three dimensions, it will result in a unique selling proposition.

What Is Your Unique Selling Proposition?

A unique selling proposition (USP) is what made F. W. Woolworth, Sam Walton, and Henry Ford wealthy men in a competitive market place. Woolworth's five-and-dime gave customers exactly what they needed—easy to remember prices for everything. Henry Ford delivered an affordable driving experience, in basic black. In the more modern era, consider Ben & Jerry, whose desire to create a company that lives out its social activist values, donates a considerable proportion of its profits to charity, yet still manages to generate robber baron-size profits from the sale of ice cream for this Vermont-based fast-food retailer and manufacturer.

OBJECTIVE: To test and validate unique selling proposition.

PROCESS: Engage customers and staff in the process of taking each dimension of your company, one at a time, and identifying the areas where you should excel and do excel.

Do the same for your competition to identify the areas where you are truly unique.

Ensure these are the words and ideas and images featured in your selling proposition. For example, if you find words such as "fast, speed, convenient, and nearby" reoccurring as you listen to customers and staff, look at some recent communications to see if they are reflected there.

TACTIC: An adjective checklist (described in Chapter Two) is an excellent way to get this information. Choosing the right words for the list is a sophisticated task, best left to psychologists and specialist research houses. These words must be easy to understand and interpreted by everyone the same way. Ask the researchers to include the words you want people to use to describe you. You and your competition should be compared using the same list of words. You're not unique if your potential customers describe you both with exactly the same words!

It is no accident that the first names that come to mind when one thinks of companies with powerful selling propositions are often ones within hailing distance of their founder. Breathing the same air as the one who made it all come to life certainly helps those working in a company to live out the contract in every dimension of the business. It is much easier to articulate the unique selling proposition and deliver a total experience when there is a single vision and a single voice.

But a single individual or a family dynasty is no guarantee of a strong selling proposition or of it being translated into three integrated dimensions. Just think of the number of department stores that didn't make it after decades of what appeared to be an unassailable vision of greatness. What is the difference between Macy's, almost brought to its knees in the leveraged-buyout-crazed '80s and Dillards, a 100-year-plus icon? What explains why the famous blue gift boxes of Birks, a Montreal-based jeweler barely survived recession under the latest generation, while at Lacks Furniture in south Texas the same economic conditions resulted in a family tradition which continues to evolve into an even stronger selling proposition for customers? It is the *focus* of the team.

Is Your Team in Focus With the USP?

In companies which survive over the long term, every employee can articulate the unique selling proposition in terms of how it affects their own job. In *The Discipline of Market Leaders*[2], Michael Treacy and Fred Wiersema help their readers understand the implications of the message "you can't be all things to all people" by providing examples of the power that occurs when a company chooses and practices a single discipline.

Dell Computer and Wal-Mart are insistent on "Operational Excellence" or getting things right the first time. Their employees know that mistakes should be prevented, not fixed, and that ideas for saving costs will be rewarded with bonuses or profit sharing. On the other hand, at 3M and Nike with their

---

[2] Michael Treacy and Fred D. Wiersema, *The Discipline of Market Leaders: Choose Your Customers, Narrow Your Focus, Dominate Your Market* (City: Addison-Wesley, 1996).

unparalleled "Product Leadership" the emphasis is placed on product. The employee who created sticky Post-it notes while doodling at his 3M desk certainly understood the focus of his company. Those who choose to practice "Customer Intimacy" such as Cable & Wireless Communications are companies where employees understand the value of taking the time to listen to customers instead of rushing to complete paperwork on time. A company that has a cadre of employees focused on a unique selling proposition is positioned to keep every dimension in harmony.

OBJECTIVE: To ensure everyone is focused.

PROCESS: Create a consistent message format in each of your key communication areas and then ensure your selling proposition is referred to as often as possible.

Make sure every document starts with "the big picture," an understanding of how this fits into the overall plan, strategy, and values.

Include the benefits for shareholders, employees, and customers. If you can't think of benefits for all three, think again. Is this really a message you want to send?

Provide the details that people need to know in order to do this or explain it to others.

TACTIC: Select any recent communication, call three people at random, and ask them the following questions about it:

Why are we doing this (what is discussed in the communication)? How does it benefit our customers, you, and the business? How does it apply to you in your everyday work?

If you get different answers, talk to your communications team about setting up a better format.

So, to be focused, first make certain that you have a unique selling proposition. To do that, you must articulate the compelling aspects of your business that define everything you do. Do you provide the widest possible selection of merchandise at everyday value pricing? Are you the leaders in low prices and lower operating costs? Are you the expert with the knowledge to answer questions?

Then, make sure your team understands the implications for them in every decision they make as they go about their work in the organization and with customers. For instance, if you are the "experts," staff must know about the product, take the time to apply this knowledge to individual customer needs, and make sure things such as the informational brochure racks are always fully stocked.

FAITHFUL: KEEP THE GOAL IN SIGHT

From our perch at the end of the century, it sometimes seems that early retailers were somehow more focused than their modern counterparts; they appear to have been outstanding leaders who set a course and stuck to it. But, one wry observer of the history of retailing describes the business of the thirties: "The retailer's uncertainty in choosing among appeals to price, quality, fashion, or staple reliability led him to try to be all things to all people. Too often, he found that he thereby weakened his ability to reach any one group."[3]

For too many companies the making of money was not a *measure* of how well they were delivering the unique selling proposition, it became the *goal*.

---

[3] Susan Porter, *Counter Cultures...Saleswomen, Managers and Customers in American Department Stores 1890–1940* (Illinois: University of Illinois Press, 1988), p. 113.

Increased Sales Are Not the Goal!

Sales are simply a measure of how well you are doing at delivering your selling proposition. In many companies, this statement would be perceived as heresy. If there is no profit, there will be no business, would be their argument. But the road to Chapter Eleven and the bankruptcy courts is paved with those who turned the making of money into their reason for being.

When making money (and then more money) becomes the primary goal, it is easy to lose touch with the selling proposition. Consider Bloomingdales, the dowager queen of midtown Manhattan. The corporate vision was to bring the best of the world to its customers in an exciting setting where shopping felt like entertainment.

Almost since its inception, "Bloomies" provided a sense of theatre in its window decoration, in-store displays, and events that were the talk of the town. When Bloomingdales ran one of their "shopping the world" furniture events, people came from far and wide to experience magnificent room settings reflecting Italy, China, or Ireland. It didn't even seem out of place when Her Majesty Queen Elizabeth II was invited to the event featuring Great Britain. Former CEO Marvin Traub talks about what it took to bring the world to a store. "Define and build the core customer by presenting the store; the merchandise; the promotions and the environment to match,"[4] he wrote. Sounds to us like he was putting the three dimensions in harmony in an execution that would deliver traffic and sales.

In recent decades, it appears that the company began to focus on the shareholder perspective, questioning the cost of this "entertainment" and whether each event generated the anticipated sales.

---

[4] Marvin Traub and Tom Teicholz, *Like No Other Store: The Bloomingdales Legend and the Revolution in American Marketing* (Random House, 1994.)

Consequently, the retailer's ads followed the rest of the industry into the land of discount prices and, along the way, some of the magic that was Bloomingdales was lost. As happened in so many other companies, the point of view that translated into a unique selling proposition dimmed and almost died. Instead of letting the making of money be a *measure* of how well they were doing things, the making of money became the *goal* and the store lost its theatre, its free publicity, and some say, its heart. Can you imagine a full-page ad inviting the Queen to attend a 50%-off sale?

So how does a company adapt its unique selling proposition in a changing world without falling into the trap of making sales the goal? They must use multiple measures from the perspectives of all three stakeholders. Gross margin or profit is the measure only for the owner/shareholder. Companies that have a strategy have a measurement system which keeps their attention on the employee and customer as well. Customer perceptions become as important as customer buying behaviour. Employee satisfaction ranks right up there with inventory turnover. And, management is evaluated on their success at preparing the organization for rapid market changes or unforeseen emergencies.

Let us tell you the story of a company which successfully created and delivered a unique selling proposition. For them the sales result remained, as it should, simply one of a series of measures, never becoming the goal.

Danier Leather: Faithful To the Goal

This company started life as The Leather Attic, a discount leather house known more for low prices than high fashion, and for many years successfully delivered the proposition inherent in that name to its customers. Today, reborn as Danier Leather, the company lives out the proposition that it should be possible for every woman to have quality leather as an integral part of her fashion-forward wardrobe. They offer Canadian women a combination of fashion, quality, and affordability. How did they achieve this major shift in approach and do the required 180-degree turn from discount to high fashion?

The company slowly and deliberately changed every aspect of all three dimensions to bring them into line with the new selling proposition. The changes ranged from colour inserts in Canada's national business newspaper in the media dimension, to brighter, larger stores and a higher quality product in the physical dimension, to a more fashion aware and informed staff in the people dimension. Throughout, they used multiple measures to track their performance. Consumer research revealed some discomfort among consumers that the shift was going to mean higher prices. The company responded by expanding the size and presence of their warehouse store to reinforce the message that, as the manufacturer, they could afford to offer both quality and affordability. And, they added this message to their media activities.

Customer reluctance to move to a higher quality and more expensive product was countered with increased product knowledge delivered by staff and an extended product guarantee. When mystery shopping revealed that staff performance was inconsistent across the country, a year-long investment in training helped to even out the results. Of course sales and profits continued to matter, but the founder and management had the long view and the staying power to invest five years to move the company away from the discount image to the fashion image they have today. They have been so successful that they are often mentioned, unprompted, in our customer focus groups as one of the top "fashion" stores in Canada.

OBJECTIVE: To keep the organization faithful to the unique selling proposition.

PROCESS: Get up from your desk and go and walk about your company.

Introduce yourself to customers and ask them what they think your company stands for.

Ask them to tell you what you do better than the competition.

Talk to the employee hired last week and the accountant who has been chained to the desk for years about the selling proposition and how you are measuring its success.

You're the leader and if you show interest in keeping the unique selling proposition alive, so will they.

TACTIC: Listen to yourself as you speak to your employees. If the first words out of your mouth always have to do with "sales results" you are focused on the scoreboard and not on what is causing you to win or lose the game.

Just like the tennis star who won't win the game by keeping his eyes on the scoreboard, the business that shifts its focus from the real objective is ultimately destined for a loss.

FLEXIBLE: USE A PENCIL NOT A PEN

You create a flexible plan by doing three things. First, involve those closest to the action in creating the plan. Second, focus everyone on outcomes, not tasks. Third, provide them with the problem solving and analytical skills to know when it is time to change.

- Traditionally, the strategy was developed in the vacuum of the executive suite, and then it trickled down to those who would actually implement it. Today, a successful business plan must consult those who are exposed daily to the requirements of the company's changing market place, the front-line employees. They are the ones with their fingers on the pulse of your business. While leadership is essential when it comes to focus, staff involvement is the key when it comes to being able to deliver a flexible environment.

- Second, focus everyone on accomplishments, not tasks. Rather than an activity orientation—"How many meetings did you attend today?"—the team should have a goal orientation. The important question is, "How did the meetings help us accomplish the goal?" There are many classic goal-setting courses or systems from which you can choose. The important thing is that every tactic or action can be evaluated against the question, "So, how is this going to help us reach our goal or objectives?"

- Everybody has to have the skills to do their own problem solving as the need arises. It is the front-line service providers who can tell you what they would do in the event of an emergency in the market place. They are the ones who can tell you what latitude they need to be able to adjust the details in the face of a competitor's action. Listen to what they have to say.

In the end, those on the selling or service floor will be held accountable for the results of this grand strategy. This is why modern strategic planning should keep the details in pencil (and an eraser handy) to allow for quick fine-tuning and revisions by those closest to the action.

> **OBJECTIVE:** To ensure the staff can be flexible.
>
> **PROCESS:** Have the staff take a look at the current goal, objectives, and tactics and create a list of all the factors which might cause dramatic change. For instance, what if the competition opened an Internet Mall store, or a major supplier went bankrupt, or several key staff members quit.
>
> Discuss how the plan could be changed without losing focus.
>
> Make sure they can tell you what resources will be required, how long things will take, and how they are going to measure the outcomes to continue to deliver the goal, even if the details of the plan have to be adjusted.
>
> **TACTICS:** Ask your training department to find you some strategy games. These can help everyone from the executive suite to the front-line understand what flexible means. Good sources for these are the local training and development association, *Training Magazine,* or the American Society of Training and Development (ASTD), both of which rate games suited to a variety of service business situations.

FAST: A QUICK TURNAROUND

The sights are set (vision, mission, values), the route's mapped (goals, objectives, and tactics), but a great strategy also demands a quick response. If tactics are not working to deliver goals, you need to know while there is still time to take action which can positively affect the results.

Too many measurements are historical. If you are waiting for sales to tell you if the plan is working, the opportunity for change is already passed. You gain speed when your front-line staff are given the feedback they need to instantly assess if the tactics or plans are working.

Here is how you create a list of real-time behaviours that influence measures for your organization. Start with an important measurement, for example, customer satisfaction. Think about the factors that could negatively affect those results: frustration if the computer system is down, employees not knowing enough about the product or service, being out of stock in a key product. Think about when these occur in the field and to whom. Make sure staff know the list and what actions they can take in real time. This is your list of real time behaviours. Some real-life examples?

A buyer noticed a lag in sales in half the stores and found that the product training had been missed in a region. She got the inventory moved to the performing stores and avoided customers being frustrated by staff who didn't know enough about the product.

The reservations clerk answered five calls in a row from customers who asked the same questions about the exact date of an upcoming local festival. Her curiosity uncovered a magazine article which was likely to bring a flood of calls. The supervisor was able to call in reinforcements and handle the unexpected enquiries and extra bookings.

Continuous training and involvement in the strategic journey will increase performance levels and allow people to take action without waiting to be told what to do next.

INVOLVE THE TEAM

Including front-line staff at the planning table allows a company to tap into the knowledge of those who deal with customers on a daily basis. It also provides the conduit to ensure that the strategy translates into the micro viewpoint. Here are things to consider when you involve your team in an overall planning process to create strategy which equips you to be focused, faithful, flexible, and fast:

- *Avoid Information Overload:* Organize the strategy planning in at least two stages. Use one session to establish the focus and big picture goals, and another session to devise a plan of action.

- *Do Your Homework:* Arm yourself with the data you need to answer the question—What is the gap between who we say we are (mission statement) and what our consumers, staff, and shareholders experience in every aspect of the business?

- *No Hierarchy Allowed:* Keep your focus-setting group small with one or two representatives from each of your dimensions and each of your stakeholders—the executive office, front-line staff, marketing people, product buyers or developers, human resources officers, shareholders.

- *Prepare Participants:* Distribute a detailed agenda well in advance to allow participants time to prepare their thoughts, data, and input.

- *Get Away From The Hurley Burley:* Book an off-site meeting room, or go on a retreat, but get the strategy session away from the distractions of the working environment.

- *Set The Tone:* A round table allows face-to-face discussions with no obvious seat of authority. Everyone's on equal ground.

- *Manageable Sound Bites:* Break up the work sessions with leisure time to let people get away and think about everything, then return with a fresh perspective.
- *An Impartial Party:* Hire an external facilitator who will keep your group focused and encourage the necessary tough discussions to take place.

Focused, Faithful, Flexible, Fast

All three stakeholders are well served by a company whose strategy can be described with these four behaviours. Shareholders know that profit and growth are being protected into the future. Employees understand their importance and can take pride in personal and team accomplishments. And customers receive a well-defined selling proposition, delivered in a variety of ways that meet their needs. Or do they? To find out how Butterfly Customers are interpreting what you offer them, you must examine the Expectations Contract they write with you.

CHAPTER EIGHT

The Expectations Contract

MISREADING THE CUSTOMER

I F A UNIQUE selling proposition is your contract with the customer, then the expectations contract is the one they make with you. It is one over which you have very little control as the customer reads and interprets your messages through a never-ending explosion of personal experiences and history.

It would be wonderful if customers were a blank page upon which you could write your message, but they're not. Everything you communicate, every experience you provide is filtered through the prism of the customer's mind. What happens when customers view you through these filters? Hidden expectations.

HIDDEN EXPECTATIONS

In a recent service seminar, an audience of marketing professionals was shown an ad for a new service from an unnamed airline. We asked the group to review the ad and then, based on what they saw and read, tell us their expectations.

The responses were generally positive. "It's a new service so I guess they will pay special attention, at least for the first while." "They talk about the new jets and service for executives so I guess they will be pretty prompt and efficient." "It's obviously aimed at business flyers so the service must be way above average." "It's higher priced."

We then revealed the name of the airline and sixty percent of the audience downgraded their expectations. Some actually became cynical as a result. For instance, the group had originally said they would be willing to pay a higher price for the level of service promised. But would they pay a higher price once they learned the name of the company? "No way" was the consensus.

One participant challenged the methodology, saying the outcome was flawed because she would never have thought so negatively about that airline if she hadn't been set up to imagine perfection.

Was she right? Did we set her up to imagine perfection or, did the ad do that? Did the methodology create unrealistic expectations? Afraid not. In fact, those are the thoughts she would have created in her subconscious had she read the ad on her own, in the privacy of her home. All the exercise did was lift up for examination at a cognitive level, thoughts that are representative of the hidden expectations that sit somewhere below the conscious level of every customer and potential customer, just waiting for the right trigger.

Unfortunately, and all too often, these expectations lurking in the subconscious are only brought to the surface when triggered by the customer taking advantage of your offer. When the gap between what they expected and what they experience is large enough, it causes the Uh-oh feeling.

To deliver a seamless experience with no shadows or Uh-ohs, you must get at those lurking thoughts while they are still deeply buried. If they are negative, you can address and fix them before they influence the customer's decision about whether or not to do business with you. On the other hand, if they are positive, you can use them to your advantage perhaps as part of your unique selling proposition.

In this chapter, we will look at a couple of research methods that will assist you in unlocking those hidden expectations found in Butterfly Customers. But first, just as important as selecting the right research techniques, is knowing what to look for. Just as the changing world creates opportunities for new products and services, the same changing world has a profound effect on humankind. While each of us is affected in a unique way, there are three key factors we have found to consistently affect customer's hidden expectations.

Competitive Chaos exposes the plethora of choices facing the customer and how the resulting confusion influences their perceptions and expectations.

Economic Atmosphere analyses the effect personal economic reality is having on the way customers respond to your business proposition.

Consumer Mood evaluates the trends in how consumers are feeling as they approach a decision to buy, or not to buy.

How these concepts converge affects how the customer approaches you, how they interpret the service contract you are offering, and how much elasticity they are prepared to give to any business.

COMPETITIVE CHAOS

One key factor in the creation of your customer's expectations is the messages they receive and the service they experience from your competition. But who is the competition?

That used to be an easy question to answer. One simply looked down the street, across the road, or on the next corner and examined the company that offered the same product or service as you did. The direct competition was the only place you had to look. But the Butterfly Customer lives in a world made chaotic by choice. In a time when customers on the Internet can browse the stores in the local mall without leaving their homes, or order from a catalogue that originated in a country halfway around the world, how far do you have to travel to check out the competition?

How far afield did Berean, the chain store presented in Chapter Six have to roam to find competitors in its market? It had to look a long way past other religious book retailers and even beyond specialized independents; going out to secular bookstores wasn't far enough. As it turned out, in some markets, the strongest influences on customer expectations came from the local supermarket. This non-traditional competitor had recently eaten into the expected sales of three key best-sellers.

To uncover the motivations of these Butterflies, Berean asked: Was it an impulse purchase? Was it perceived as more or less expensive than at Berean? Was it simply easier to piggyback this purchase onto the grocery list? Was it a faster, more efficient purchase? Was it a "small indulgence" reward for surviving the grocery shopping experience? If they hadn't found the competitor they wouldn't have been able to adjust their delivery to better meet the customer expectations. In this case, all it took was some redesign at the cash to allow for more impulse purchases. And what better place to learn how to do that than from the masters in the grocery business.

Imagine, competitors you don't even know are determining your relationship with the customer and the evidence of blurring boundaries when it comes to who sells what is found everywhere. The supermarket dispenses drugs, bookstores sell coffee, and clothing chains market home accessories. Service stations become mini-supermarkets where the busy Butterfly fills up the fridge as well as the car, and hospitals feature specialty stores selling a lot more than just gifts for the sick in their high-traffic lobbies.

Knowing all the nooks and crannies which contain competitors is a continuing challenge but one worth pursuing. It's cheap research because it can be done quickly and accurately by your front-line employees.

OBJECTIVE: Seek customer and staff help in finding out who is the competition.

PROCESS: On your regular visits to the front lines, ask your customers to tell you of any other sources which supply your product or service, or one similar.

Ask customers about their favourite places to spend any disposable income. Your competition may be someone who offers a better experience, not a better product or service.

TACTIC: Use staff to check out these nearby competitors and see why they might appeal to customers.

Share local perspectives in a regional or national forum on the phone, or in person, or over a company-owned Intranet (a secure, private internet line, suitable for private information).

Make timely and accurate identification and evaluation of competition a part of every job description in the company.

Once you are sure you have identified those places your customer thinks of as competition and you have experienced them yourself, it is time to explore how you react to competitors and how those reactions could affect how the customer feels about you.

You Ignore the Competition

One client who owned a ski shop held dearly to the notion that his customers were the "serious skiers" and if they wanted the latest ski equipment and the most accurate product information and boot fitting techniques, then he was the only choice. But as customer counts dribbled downward (even during the years that skiing increased in popularity), he began to take another look.

Why were his customers abandoning him? Because he treated them as if the competition didn't exist. While he was continuing to do business as usual, the competition had improved service levels, increased staff expertise, and created customer-friendly policies. A quick evaluation uncovered a serious shift in the competition's performance compared to his. He charged for binding adjustments (after all, his people did the best adjustments in the territory) while the competition now adjusted bindings free. Returning clothing to his store was a challenge but the competition had implemented a no-questions-asked policy. The result? Serious skiers still came to him but only bought their "serious" ski stuff from him. Unfortunately, that was the stuff that required high levels of customer service and staff attention. Most of their high-margin, low-maintenance, big-dollar business went elsewhere.

Once the retailer understood that he couldn't afford to ignore the competition he quickly moved to adjust those annoying policies which, in fact, had been contributing very little revenue, and regained the loyalty of a core of loyal Monarchs.

You Blindly Follow the Competition

Just as disconcerting to the Butterfly Customer is a company that responds to competitive challenges by blindly following the leader and constantly fiddling with their policies and operation. The resulting "New!" "Improved!" "More for less!" slogans cause the Butterfly Customer to quietly ask: "If it's new and improved now, what was it before?" or "If it's cheaper now does that mean you were ripping me off all those years at the old price?" In an attempt to combat the inroads into the market by the new breed of discounters, and no-name products, many icons, such as Bloomingdales (as we saw in the previous chapter), have lost out by being too imitative of the competition.

Sears learned this lesson the hard way. In 1989 they closed down the entire chain for forty-eight hours to "lower the price on all the products" in response to the Wal-Mart challenge of every-day low prices. But many Sears customers we spoke to said they thought Sears already had some of the best prices in town. So how could these customers continue to deal with a company that, in essence, declared they had been making too much money on too many products? They flew away in droves but fortunately they were, at heart, Monarchs and, after a period of flitting about the competition, began to return to their natural home. Recent operating profits and growth rates confirm the story that Sears has regained the trust of their customers.

Make certain you are not jumping on the competitor's bandwagon without fully understanding how your response will be interpreted by your customers.

OBJECTIVE: Verify that your response to the competitive challenge is appropriate.

PROCESS: Having identified the competitive offerings, evaluate your customer's perspective of these and how they compare you to them.

Present your selling proposition as it exists today and determine the emotions this position creates in customers.

Next, present your revised proposition and determine the emotions this change creates in customers.

TACTIC: In the research, make sure you include customers who used to be yours and aren't any longer.

THE ECONOMIC ATMOSPHERE

The second element that affects customer behaviour is the economic atmosphere. But this is more than just the economic facts about your operating environment. It is how those facts are making your customers feel. Perhaps the best way to illustrate this is to look at what we are seeing in our market place at the time this book is published.

In the mid-nineties in North America, something has shaken the faith of customers to such a degree that, for the first time, researchers such as Alan Gregg of Decima Research reported uncovering a group of customers who said they wanted a certain product or service, maybe even needed it, had the money to acquire it, yet they *still did not make the purchase*.[1] This is no longer a financial decision, but an emotional one caused by the economic atmosphere.

---

[1] Allan Gregg, Decima Research; Retail Council of Canada Annual Convention Proceedings, 1994.

Even though the economy in North America has recently shown some strength, the atmosphere has changed and that change effects the customer. The customer is no longer sure about their economic security. When the executive living next door to you is afraid of losing her job and the retired couple across the street are dipping into their savings and worrying about the next government tax grab, they are not going to spend even if they want, need, and can afford the product.

What is the moral of the story for the business that wants to stay in touch with the economic atmosphere of their customers? Pay attention to how much money customers *feel* they have, not how much they actually *do* have.

Making Do

"Just making do" is how the Butterfly Customer is feeling about the economic atmosphere. How does it affect their feelings as they approach your business and what can you do about it? Today's consumers may be the first since our grandmothers to make purchases designed, not for the planned obsolescence of the '80s, but to last a decade. Making do is often misread as a need to buy cheaper when, in fact, buying a higher quality, higher priced item or service may satisfy this need just as well.

So don't just respond with discounts. Find creative ways to help the customer get the most out of their investment with you. You must seek ways to be their partner in making do. Here are three ideas to help you help them.

1. Take a look at your post-sales service, warranties, and other policies designed to help a product last a long time. The move in the auto industry to offer longer and more-inclusive warranties is one example of the positive response to the economic atmosphere of making do.

2. The second-hand market is another area where making do has an impact. If you want your customer to buy new, help them trade-in or convert what they have to cash. If the image of running a permanent garage sale in your warehouse has little appeal, there are many other ways to do this. The explosion of second-hand stores from Value Village to Play it Again Sports and others in the the used computer field offer you a chance to help your customer. You might work out a deal with one of these retailers to give your customers a discount coupon, or, you could situate your store in a mall near one of theirs.

3. When you offer the client the best long-term value, make sure your staff have the product knowledge to communicate the proposition. While the customer wants to buy as an investment, dollars are still tight and any major purchasers are considered very carefully. Give your staff the level of knowledge they need to satisfy this intense customer scrutiny.

TIP

> **OBJECTIVE:** To understand how much money customers feel they have.
>
> **PROCESS:** Intersperse your business reading with consumer stories. Track the number of articles appearing about "101 ways to stretch hamburger" versus "Entertaining like royalty."
>
> Read some trend books and articles and subscribe to "moods" research which explores how customers are feeling, not just what they are doing.
>
> **TACTIC:** This is one case where "know thyself," and know thy customer will be very helpful. Find friends and family who match the profile of your customers, and get them talking about how "poor" or "rich" they are feeling and acting.

THE CONSUMER MOODS

What your company brings to the market place will be interpreted by customers through the chaos of choice, the economic atmosphere, and one more important filter—the trends in consumer moods. Reading the consumer mood and anticipating the swings is a critical skill for a company that wants to create loyalty with the Butterfly Customer. It is not just knowing what customers want, it is understanding why they want it that can help a company serve all the moods, and be poised to handle any swings.

For instance, when consumers feel as if they are making do, as previously discussed in Economic Atmosphere, then prestige-laden brand names will hold little appeal unless you help them see how this purchase will benefit them by providing a long-lasting product.

How do you find out what the trend is when it comes to consumer moods? Join the popular gurus who make it their business to study consumers all the time. Most of the major research houses in North America offer a variety of regular reports, including consumer mood studies, and will be pleased to send you the information. Increasingly, industry associations also sponsor major studies into how consumers are feeling about doing business with you. The National Retail Federation is just one such annual trend-watcher.

In addition to the making do trend discussed earlier, there are three others which should be considered when formulating strategy or making plans in any of the three dimensions.

Reward me: In no matter how small a way, the consumer is determined to reward themselves for having survived.

In Control!: The desire to take charge of something, anything in a gyroscopic, topsy-turvy world.

No Time: The increasing realization that this is one resource which can only be depleted.

Reward Me

This motive is about deserving a reward for surviving the battle. It can result in the purchase of the $3.00 chocolate truffle, a $30 bottle of wine, or a $300 custom silk shirt. What Faith Popcorn has called "small indulgences" is part of this, but it includes far more than an indulgence. It is a reward for hard work and making do.

The "reward me" motive responds to the company that throws in something extra, or offers a real, but (an almost unbelievable) value. Here are two practical ways to do it.

1. If your wholesaler offers you a fantastic bargain, say an item that is "worth" $200 retail for a mere $10, think hard about what kind of deal you want to offer your customers. Maybe this is a case where a selling price of $50 brings you a very nice margin and your customer a handsome saving. Win/win is never more important than when dealing with this mood.

2. Create offers that, for just a few dollars more, allow a whole lot more reward. One ski resort lets kids under 17 stay and ski for free. This is a real reward, and they are booked for the entire season by mid-December.

Tell customers you know they are survivors and you are ready to help them reward themselves. Two companies who say it well? The good old McDonald's restaurant slogan "You Deserve A Break Today" is a message to this mood and so is the L'Oréal "I'm Worth It" campaign.

In Control

Considering the number of times the consumer ends up paying the price for believing superficial "expertise" provided by some corporation, it is no wonder that today's customer wants control. It's the only way to ensure security.

The Butterfly Customer doesn't want generic answers or preformatted solutions, they want information that allows them to make their own decisions. They want the details and facts that will let them form a personal answer or strategy.

1. Tell the truth, even if it hurts. One Canadian company built a strong brand loyalty by appealing to this mood. Buckley's cough syrup slogan said, "It tastes awful, but it works." One Internet provider shares a constantly updated list of the top ten reasons customers call their customer support. Reason #8 on the list? "To cancel the service." This is the fastest growing provider in North America. It doesn't bother most customers to know that a few want to quit the service.

2. We don't think it's any accident that "options" are creeping back into the car market. Customers want to select the package that suits them, not the manufacturer. Saturn is perhaps the best known and best example of designing a business proposition for the customer who wants to be in control. Not only do they separately list every option and let the customer decide which ones they want, they even produce a straightforward price list.

No Time

Time has always been a precious commodity and millions of retailers and service providers built their businesses around the notion of convenience and time saving. What do you do to respond to this mood?

If the media message promises "fast" service, or "quick" response, you better be sure you know just what fast and quick means to your customer, and that you can deliver. Take an audit of your business and look for all the ways you hint at or outright offer time saving. The words "fast, drive through, automatic, efficient" all imply rapid service but do they meet the customer's expectation of rapid? Have you found yourself in a line-up at the automatic teller machine lately? What about waiting for the car to fill-up at the gas station—just why are the pumps used by attendents twice the speed of yours?

If you want to assess how fast you really are, you need to put on the customer's watch and passively wait through your experience. It is amazing how long a minute is when you have nothing to do.

But there is a new element of time beyond that of convenience, and that is that "time is running out." David Foot, noted Canadian economist and demographer, uses the mantra "Every year we get one year older" in his books and speeches to engage his audiences in the powerful moods created by the relentless progression of the "boom bulge" through the century. This twenty-year spike in the birth rate following the end of the Second World War causes a heightened response to every life passage. From the youth cults of the '60s to the focus on the family of the present day, where boomers are in life affects the mood of the entire market place. What are we seeing in response to the moodiness felt by boomers whose personal clock reads mid-life?

In addition to the plethora of products designed to get the entire world saving for their retirement, we are seeing a willingness to discuss issues from caring for aging parents to proctology that would have been unmentionable even a decade ago. Media messages and customers questions are no longer skirting subjects that were once taboo, from adult diapers to balding remedies. Here are some other ways this mood is affecting behaviour.

1. The heirloom business will return as people buy their "last" piece of furniture or jewellery. Not only will it need to be durable, it will need to be beautiful to pass the generational test.

2. People will buy comfort over fashion or fad in products and services. While it will be decades before adult walkers outsell baby strollers, in the meantime, bunions and aging backs will mean changes in shoes, fitting rooms, and airline seats.

In this era when time of both kinds is now *more* valuable than money, understanding your relationship to this customer mood is critical.

WHAT IS MY CUSTOMER FEELING TODAY?

To create loyalty with the Butterfly Customer, you had better pay attention to the entire spectrum of factors which affect how the customer is feeling even before approaching your business. So, if competition, the economic atmosphere, and consumer moods all influence your customer's expectations, how do you find out which influences are dominant today?

Let's look at two common emotional research techniques that can be powerful sources to unlock customer emotions: focus groups and behavioural observations.

Focus Groups

During a recent flight to Chicago, the vice-president of marketing in the adjoining seat spent nearly an hour explaining why he had abandoned focus groups as a research technique. Among his compelling reasons: "the group gets dominated by a single point of view; customers don't care enough to tell you what they really think; there are too few opinions to make any real decisions."

We couldn't agree more. So why do we conduct so many focus groups each year? Because if they are designed to gather feelings, not opinions, they work very well indeed.

What is the difference between opinion-seeking and feeling-seeking groups? The former tend to start with a point of view and use strategies designed to get at the customers' response to that point of view. The latter are designed to take customers into their real world and uncover the feelings that create their personal point of view.

Here is a story of how a "feeling" focus group worked for one customer faced with declining customer counts. Previous research had found that customers still described the business in positive terms but were vague about recent promotions. Based on this finding it is not surprising to learn that the marketing department suggested that the company use its database to invite these "loyal" customers back in communications that featured and explained the recent promotions. When the mailing failed to yield the desired results, it was time for a closer look.

What did we do to "feel" the reasons for the customers' behaviour? In the first research, customers had been asked to create photo collages of the business. The photos they chose all featured crowds: line-ups at the cash, lots of shoppers in the store, customers with no staff in sight. And, they did not choose any photos showing customers receiving attentive service.

We took this original research one step further. Customers were shown these collages and asked what they thought the people in the pictures were thinking and feeling as they waited in line, were served, and left. We uncovered some real anger. Customers seethed, "Don't they think my time has any value?" and "It's a good thing their prices are so low. It wouldn't be worth it otherwise."

No wonder the invitations didn't work. It turned out the problem was not in the media dimension but in the people dimension. Further searching uncovered that, in fact, there was a sufficient staff to customer ratio but because of recent staff turnover, too many customers were being served by staff who were inexperienced and thus slow.

A Focus Group Primer

There are many excellent marketing and research companies who do this type of research, but even a professional may not have the skills or insights to create a feeling focus group. Here are a series of questions that can help you evaluate a focus group plan brought to you by your own team or an outside professional.

- What evidence is there in their plan that proves the objective of the research is to understand how customers feel and why?

- Is the sample group the right one to tell you things you don't already know? Make sure it is not selected only from current customers and demographic segments, but represents competitors' customers and varying psychographics.

- Is the focus group moderator skilled at dealing with conceptual and emotional issues? Check references and make sure their experience includes researching a broader range of issues than just new products or advertising campaigns.

- Are all of the specifics of the list of issues (what you want to find out) related to the customers' emotions? If you want to check demographic facts or buying patterns, a survey might be a better, and cheaper, way to go. Don't forget to include issues from all three dimensions. You want to explore their reaction to the integrated experience, not just one aspect.

- Can the team tell you how the exercises and techniques they have selected will get customers expressing their feelings? Ask how they know and listen for insight and intelligence about customer psychology and the skill of writing good research questions.

Focus groups are a great way to feel the mood of the customer. But a large percentage of communication is non-verbal, such as the tone of voice, facial expressions, and body language.

Behavioural observations are the technique we use to explore this aspect of how the customer feels.

Behavioural Observations

The problem with interviewing customers is they use words and phrases that may mean one thing to you but another to them. We have found that one way to overcome that barrier is to watch customers as they interact with your setting before we interview them.

A trained observer tracks customers as they phone in an order, surf a Web site, walk through the store, use an automatic teller or ticketing machine, or partake of your service experience. All the details of the experience are noted, including things such as looking, pausing, touching, paying, or waiting. The observer records the patterns of customer traffic, that is, where each customer went first and how long they stayed at each location. At the conclusion of the observation, the customer is asked a series of questions about the experience which are then compared to the actions.

Over hundreds of such observations, there is a great deal to be learned about the difference between what customers say and what they actually do. Some customers claim to love being served, but in fact, respond with negative body language when approached directly by a service person. Others will tell the researcher how much they liked the product display while the observation clearly recorded a facial expression of confusion or distaste. We watch customers spend an inordinate amount of time looking at signs, playing with displays, and reading product literature only to learn that they can't remember what they saw, or explain what they learned in the interview. The value of behavioural observation is not limited to learning about the customer but provides an opportunity to evaluate building design, merchandise display, and presentation. It allows the researcher to feel the experience from the point of view of both the staff and the customer.

Observing Customers Buy Greeting Cards

Summit Corporation, the umbrella retail operation for Carlton Cards, the product brand, wanted to explore ways to use the positive feelings about the Carlton brand's consistency and quality to create positive associations with the corporate store. In a test, they added the Carlton brand name on the store sign and organized the displays by brand.

They then asked us to take a closer look at the impact on the customer and staff. What we found was a mixed blessing. On the one hand, customers displayed positive body language, pausing longer at the brand displays in the new, reorganized stores, and in the follow-up questions, demonstrated a higher degree of awareness of all the Carlton products in those stores. However, they ranked the level of service lower in the branded stores than in the non-branded stores, even though our observers noted no significant differences.

What had happened was that the brand name carried not only an association of the quality of the product, it also increased the expectation around the service. Exactly the same behaviour that earned acceptable ratings in a "no-name" card store did not meet customer standards in a Carlton Store. One of the solutions was a staff orientation and training program that featured the brand history, product knowledge, and a different approach to selling the brand.

Focus groups and behavioural observations are two successful methods of getting at what the customer thinks, and will help you examine how your product or service is being received by customers. What expectations contract will they write with your business based on how they are feeling about the competition and the economy? How does the consumer mood affect how customers approach your product, service, or industry?

OBJECTIVE: To set up a behavioural observation program.

PROCESS: Select two or maximum three issues about which you want to learn.

We generally focus on process (cash or service desk) and learning (displays or kiosk) and people (selling and service behaviour).

TACTIC: Your observers are going to watch the customers the entire time they are in the store, recording all they do, including any interaction with the staff. A floor plan of your location is used to plot the customer's route and any areas where time is spent.

The tracked customer is intercepted at the exit and asked a series of questions, which will vary depending on what they did during the interaction.

When the results of the observation are compared to the exit interview questions, a skilled researcher can identify any gaps.

Creating a match between what you want to sell and how you want to sell it versus what customers are in the mood to experience is a prerequisite to earning trust from the Butterfly Customer.

But it's only step one. Now, you must take a more active role in managing the expectations of your customers. In the media, physical, and people dimensions you are in charge of what you tell your customers to expect and how closely their experience matches those expectations. In the next three chapters, we explore each of the dimensions and how companies can communicate and deliver an experience which creates or maintains trust and leads to a relationship with the Monarch Customer.

The Media

THOSE SPINNERS OF magic in the ad biz do a great job of coming up with exciting, moving, and creative ways to send the message and entice the customer to visit the business.

Just think about some of the memorable campaigns designed to create a call to action. "Come see the softer side of Sears" is an invitation to explore the store beyond the traditional Craftsmen tools or automotive departments. United Airlines invites customers to "Fly the Friendly Skies" and McDonald's invites the entire family to take a well-deserved break today—with them, of course.

Launching a creative campaign takes so much focus and energy that there is a natural tendency, once it is underway, to sit back, take a deep breath, and wait for the results. And usually they are not long in coming. Well constructed media messages seldom fail in their objective of attracting the customer. In fact, what often happens is that the message is so compelling it succeeds *too well* in telling a magical tale and creating an attractive offer that is so far from reality it becomes a fatal attraction to all those customers who, like the ships responding to the siren's song, are drawn to the rocks and a watery grave.

Sales results or customer satisfaction ratings fail to deliver the expected return on investment from gloriously creative and imaginative messages. Or, the surge in the numbers is so brief it barely outlasts the campaign period. The effect is devastating, on Butterfly and business alike. When the media acts as a fatal attraction, no one wins.

GLASSES FOR THE MASSES

Let us tell you a story of a campaign that should have worked, according to any Clio[1] standards we know.

It is the early '90s and everyone in the optical industry is counting the days until all those boomers born forty years ago start buying reading glasses. This was definitely going to be *the* growth segment in the coming decade. Our client determined that the right strategy for business success was to create a selling proposition that would appeal specifically to these first-time purchasers.

Some creative research into feelings revealed that, from a consumer's point of view, buying glasses is rather like going to the dentist. This essential chore is seldom approached with anticipatory delight. The generally negative, or at best neutral, tone from consumers was exacerbated when focus group discussion turned to the factor which caused the need in the first place...aging. First time buyers in their forties emphatically did not want to be reminded of medicine, doctors, or growing old at the optical store.

They were also quite wary of the experience. They didn't know what to expect and were unsure of how the products were priced, although one recent purchaser opined, "When she gave me the total price I took a second look to see if that metal in the

---

[1] The advertising industry's award to itself for outstanding creative performance.

frames was actually gold. It should have been at that price."
Sticker-shock, or the surprise at the cost of something they
weren't keen to buy in the first place turned out to be a significant characteristic of this consumer.

An "image" campaign was designed to appeal to all these new
eye wear customers. A host of easily recognizable celebrities, all
over 30, from the world of entertainment and politics looked out
from giant-sized posters through their designer glasses and invited customers to join them in wearing beautiful eye wear.

As the advertising dollars flowed out and the sales dollars
trickled in, it soon became apparent that something had gone
wrong and large gaps had opened between listening to the consumers' voices, the creation of the media campaign, and the
experience of the sale. What did we uncover when we experienced the business feelingly?

1. The media campaign didn't meet all the needs of the business.

   This chain had suffered a series of losses and was facing stiff
   price competition. There was a strong emphasis on financial
   discipline and a constant stream of communications to the
   stores about achieving sales goals and cutting costs. The
   campaign, with its primary focus on developing a new business segment, neglected the need to develop additional sales
   from the existing customer base.

2. There was a gap between the campaign goal and tactics.

   While the campaign was a long-view program designed to
   educate and create customers, it was designed in six-week
   promotion cycles. Tactics changed so rapidly that before one
   new consumer message had a chance to sink in, the next was
   upon them.

   This approach, in fact, was better suited to a campaign
   whose goal was to increase repeat behaviour (and sales) from

the existing customer base. The only problem was, the message didn't match the needs of these consumers.

3. The team was not singing from the same song sheet.

   If anyone had asked the staff before the final campaign was developed, they could have expressed their opinion that while it might meet long-term strategy, it wouldn't do enough for the immediate cash-flow needs. The team found the entire initiative less than useful in attracting what they considered their core customers, who, as long-time eye wear users, were motivated by a combination of price and security. The retailer needed the volume of business represented by these customers to meet the immediate need to generate cash flow.

4. The media message was not matched in the other two dimensions.

   The tactics of a six-week rotating campaign were difficult to implement with current staff levels. In the physical dimension, the execution fell apart as stores failed to change signs in time to match billboards, and product displays sometimes arrived late or incomplete. In the people dimension, staff were not consistently familiar with the details of current offerings. A training program designed to help opticians stress fashion over the medical aspects for customers, did not significantly change the staff behaviour. Too many customers, attracted by the promise of designer eyewear, were greeted with, "And may I see your prescription, please!"

   At the same time, the competition launched a huge 50%-off program that all but demoralized staff who still believed their core customer, the one who could help them make those sales numbers, was motivated by price.

A focus on only one element of the business strategy, little apparent match between rapid-fire campaign tactics and a long-term goal, a staff who had not been sufficiently educated about the implications of the changes in direction, and an inability to deliver the glowing promise of the ads, threw the entire campaign into a downward spiral. And it wasn't just sales that were affected. The fatal attraction caused both old and new customers alike to flit to the competition, while staff were frustrated and confused by the mixed messages.

If you want your investment in the media dimension to create a genuinely attractive offer you must deliver:

1. A campaign which supports corporate strategy

2. No gap between the media tactics and the campaign goal

3. An involved and committed team

4. A 3-D match

Let us take a look at these requirements and how companies can shift behaviour to convert their messages from fatal attractions into attractive offers.

A CAMPAIGN WHICH SUPPORTS CORPORATE STRATEGY

The campaign must deliver the total corporate strategy. Take, for example, one client whose long-term strategy had been to develop a loyal customer base. Because what they sold was widely available, they knew that they needed customers who would return to them by choice. A key element of the strategy had been the creation of customer loyalty programs. They also needed strong profits as, in this competitive sector, a heavy investment in new technology would shortly be required.

When a senior executive finally took the time to count up all the programs and analyse their effect on the business, he was dismayed to find that an estimated ten percent of gross revenue had been given away in the previous year in this attempt to gain loyalty. Was it worth it? Would the company meet its strategic objectives by continuing to provide all of these "rewards" for customers?

By speaking to staff and observing customer interactions, the executive quickly realized that the value of the discounts to either customers or staff bore little relationship to the real cost to the company. Staff offered the discount to *any* customer, loyal, repeat, first time, it didn't matter. The program designed to reward Monarch Customers had metamorphosed into a selling tool in the hands of untrained sales associates. The irony was that when surveyed, the staff who were giving away all this gross margin resented the programs themselves! They reported that having to deal with all of these different programs slowed down the transaction as customers were kept waiting during awkward processes.

And customers concurred with staff. "It's not really a discount. They jack up the prices and then give you something off." Customers couldn't tell us why they got the discount and in fact many of them believed they were still paying higher prices than they would at the competition.

So here was a company that thought it was building profit and market share by rewarding loyal customers but in fact was: giving away shareholder profits, causing employees to lose productivity, and leaving customers feeling cheated, not rewarded.

A plan was created to align the tactics to the total corporate objective: building loyal customers while ensuring the capital to invest in new technology. Service standards were improved by training all employees. Staff were also trained to evaluate the competition and report their findings regularly. In the physical dimension, stores were spruced up and standards for housekeeping raised. Only with these dimensions in place was a media campaign, which featured the service experience, not price, launched. The new initiatives were funded from the dismantled discount programs, and within a year, the company was able to report both increased repeat visits and the kind of profits which would allow for reinvestment.

OBJECTIVE: To ensure the media campaign is aligned with the strategic needs of the organization.

PROCESS: Test the campaign against the needs of all three stakeholders. Will each receive a measurable benefit?

TACTIC: A new direction requires a close look at the impact on the core business. In the case of the optical business cited earlier, taking into consideration the price needs of long-time eyewear users resulted in the creation of a modular price format. Customers could pick and choose which elements they wanted and then receive a "package" or discounted price. Happily, this also met requirements of the new target customer for plenty of information about how the product was priced.

One way of preventing a fatal attraction is to ensure any campaign supports the total corporate strategy, and thus meets the needs of all three stakeholders. Equally important is the next element: making sure all of the tactics are supporting the goal.

NO GAP BETWEEN THE MEDIA TACTICS AND THE CAMPAIGN GOAL

Here is how one of our clients ensured that a key campaign was supported by appropriate tactics. Apple Computer customers are like those who own (or once owned) a Volkswagen. They are loyal Monarchs, almost fanatically so, and consider themselves part of an elite, in-the-know coterie. One of the most significant findings of a 3-D Audit conducted in the fall of 1995 was a softening in this core group of Apple loyalists as they considered alternative options for the first time. Also, retailers were beginning to question Apple. Some former Apple-only specialty dealers had added other brands, and the space devoted to Apple in some major retailers was on the decline.

Finally, the splashy launch of Microsoft's Windows 95 created a new image for the consumer, and stores reported that customers were now coming in to ask for a "Windows" computer. Although the core Apple customer was out there saying that "Windows 95 was equal to Apple in 86," the potential for an erosion in this valuable client base was evident.

An internal team determined that the focus of the next campaign needed to be on the protection of the brand and maintaining the loyalty of the existing core customer. This meant featuring the positive benefits of remaining an Apple customer or retailer. The advertising agency (which took part in all of the strategy sessions) created a campaign theme that delivered the selling proposition to customers and retailers alike. "Everyone is a winner at Apple."

The team created a goal to measure the campaign, along with objectives for every dimension of the business, and set about ensuring every tactic would match the campaign goal. A key component of the plan was leveraging the media dollars through co-op programs with the re-sellers designed to reinforce the "Everyone is a winner" message. Retail account representatives were provided with mock-ups of the ads well in advance of their release so that they were able to schedule appointments with their clients to inform them of the strategy and sell them on co-op participation not only in terms of dollars, but also in terms of creative energy.

One retail chain created their own in-store poster which reflected the message in over 100 stores across the nation. The planning process itself allowed the company to focus scarce resources wisely and have sufficient time to act. And more important than the positive sales results (which after all are only a measure of success in other endeavours), pre- and post-consumer and retailer surveys and testing showed an improvement in brand awareness and confidence in Apple. The company was now positioned to build its following year plan on a stronger loyal base.

OBJECTIVE: To ensure tactics match the media goal.

PROCESS: Ensure all of those connected with creating and delivering messages understand the goal of the campaign.
Think of all the aspects of the media dimension, not just the obvious ones. Signs, commercials and billboards, word of mouth, employee recommendations, and public relations should all be considered.

TACTIC: What retailers say to their consumers has an influence on how they feel about a product. Apple made it easy for retail staff to consistently reinforce the messages in the campaign by providing them pocket cards which summarized the key points of the promotion: who would "win" (every purchaser, by sending in a coupon), and how to register for a chance to "win" a grand prize (automatically).

As a team of synchronized swimmers demonstrates, it takes every member, performing the same routine to the same music in a synchronized way, to win the Olympic gold. To synchronize your team, you must first make sure there is commitment to the direction and tone of the campaign and that they are able to deliver an exactly matched message in the physical and media dimensions. But, how do you create an involved and committed team?

AN INVOLVED AND COMMITTED TEAM

Large gaps often exist between what management claims they "told" the front-line employees and what the employees say they heard, and so we spend a goodly amount of time investigating how information is communicated. Here is one client's story.

> *Last-minute changes in an important campaign were communicated during an annual sales meeting. The president of the company shared the information with the group, who internalized the message several different ways. With a crowded agenda, there was little time for questions before a scheduled break when the store managers scurried to the phones to pass the information to their assistants back in the stores.*
>
> *There was clearly going to be a gap in perceptions around this campaign. There was no "checking" to ensure everyone would be singing from the same song sheet when they transmitted the plans to their assistant managers. Gap One!*
>
> *These messages would be transmitted one more time as the assistant managers developed their own interpretations and delivered plans to the front-line staff. Gap Two!*
>
> *When we followed this campaign into the field, it was not surprising that we heard many different explanations about the promotion from staff and even more from customers interviewed as they left the stores. Gap Three—you're out!*

To avoid striking out with the team, there are three simple things you can do.

- First, involve front-line staff before the ink is dry.

  Staff are often aware of subtle customer reactions which may be missed by the creative team. As we have discussed, customers often camouflage their true feelings in opinion focus groups, but staff are on the spot, hearing the sighs as customers experience a disappointment or watching the tapping of impatient fingers as customers wait for a "free" offer to be processed at the cash. What a waste of market intelligence not to have talked to front-line people before designing (or adjusting) an expensive campaign.

- Second, provide a big picture understanding of the message and how it fits with corporate strategy.

  When the field understand the thinking behind what you are communicating to customers they can reinforce it in their own interactions with customers.

  Rahola is a chain of camera and photofinishing stores in Puerto Rico owned by Kodak. We happened to be interviewing staff there when Kodak Gold film was introduced. Staff reactions ranged from "I can't figure out why they would name a new film 'Gold' when customers already complain that Kodak film is too expensive" to "Why is the campaign on radio where you can't see a picture?" These were clear indicators that the new product hadn't been marketed to the staff before giving them the responsibility of supporting it to customers.

  Staff needed to understand why Gold was exactly the right message to take to the market place. Gold signifies value and with the possibility of Kodak's Olympic sponsorship around the corner, this was a strategic move to get ready to promote a powerful brand name and image. Had the staff understood the strategy and benefits of the product, they would have been able to internalize the message and provide customers with more positive comments about the campaign. In fact, they could have used the valuable time spent questioning the validity of the product name to promote it to the customers, probably selling a lot more film in the process.

- Third, make sure someone has thought about, and taken into consideration, how this is going to work on the front lines.

Staff are the ones who suffer the implementation headaches of yet one more creative, but unworkable, campaign. Time and time again we hear the same story: The head office gang looks at total sales results and declares "another successful campaign" while the field people look at their payroll hour budgets which soared out of sight as they struggled to hang signs, reorganize the premises, and make sure everyone is outfitted with the special T-shirt and badge in time for a promotion's start date.

Stanley Marcus (of Neiman Marcus fame) lamented the day when buyers and merchants got computers, because it kept them from getting out on the selling floor to "experience" the sale or promotion they planned. And he was right! It's time to put them back out on the floor. Recently, while doing a walk about in a major department store in the middle of a glove promotion, we took a look at the department. Customers were lined up two deep on both sides of a cash desk, each holding multiple pairs of gloves. We watched frustration grow, and eventually about 20% of the customers threw down gloves (and add-on scarves and hats) and left the store. The merchandise manager, glued to a computer screen, would only have seen product streaming out the door. Too bad. What we saw were customers leaving (maybe never to return), a poor beleaguered cashier trying vainly to cope, and a program that achieved only some small percentage of its potential in terms of sales and even less in terms of customer loyalty.

So, before you implement your plans, make sure that the creative team has talked through how this is going to be implemented in the field. Will there be an impact on staffing? What will happen to the terrific display as it is mauled over by excited customers? Will the computer go into overload when it is bombarded with customer orders? Do staff have the tools and time to put up the display and hang the signs?

The final, and perhaps most critical piece, is to ensure you can deliver a physical and people dimension which exactly match the expectations you are creating in the media dimension.

A 3-D MATCH

Unfortunately all too many businesses start out with a strong theme in their media dimension only to have it fall into discord as the initial promise fails to be delivered in the customer's experience.

Your Delivery Is Your Message, So Check First

There are hundreds of examples of media messages that customers interpreted into some quite concrete, if unarticulated, expectations, which were then found wanting when measured against the reality of delivery. Here is one example that we are not the only customers to note.

We love our American Express cards. More than once the unlimited credit line has allowed an unplanned purchase and, as small-business owners, we count on the quarterly statements to help us manage our expenses.

But, we join with many other customers in being astonished at the gap between the media promise of a technology so powerful that a replacement for a card lost in Bora Bora is delivered to a deckchair within hours, and the reality of our own mailbox.

If Amex is technologically sophisticated enough to guarantee payment of a room for a customer even though he doesn't have his card (Fall '96), why can't their computer tell them we are already a member?

Not once, but several times a year, the mailbox has contained both invitations to spend membership points *and* a form letter cajoling us to experience the benefits of membership. Their message that we have been pre-approved also disconcerts customers. As one focus group member said, "If they check to pre-approve my credit, don't they uncover the fact that I already have an account"?

These are very clear expectations built by the customer from explicit and implicit advertising messages that are jolted by the delivery. Whether it's via a fancy television commercial, your Internet Web site, a new package design, or a hand-lettered sign in the store, every time and in every way you communicate, you are setting up expectations for the customer's experience. Whether you meant to or not, you are making a contractual promise to your customers.

You must determine in advance what promises you are creating through your media, and understand the implications for the physical and people dimensions. To check expectations, make sure your research team is focused not just on the comprehension of the message, but the feelings and hidden expectations it creates. Don't forget the opportunity to involve staff at this stage. Not only will you create a synchronized team, you will be contributing to a team which knows how to deliver, and how to take advantage of the expenditures in the media dimension. And, you might just be pleasantly surprised at how the contribution of front-line staff improves your offering.

After hearing from customers and staff you are ready to walk in their shoes through the physical and people dimensions, ensuring everything lines up. Watch for any gaps or shadows and adjust your plans accordingly.

OBJECTIVE: To ensure a 3-D Match.

PROCESS: With customer and staff expectations created in the media dimension in mind, approach each of the other two dimensions.

For instance, in the physical dimension if your ad featured a brand name product, are these prominently displayed so they are the first thing customers see.

In the people dimension, ask staff the questions customers might: Where will I find the product? What do I have to do to enter the contest?

TACTIC: Do a test with a site which is far from you. Send them the information package and then call and ask questions. It is amazing how poor one-way communication can be. One restaurant chain we know uses a "hot-line" which is open during those late-evening hours when the staff might need questions answered as they prepare for the next day's promotional event.

GUARDING AGAINST CREATING A FATAL ATTRACTION

If you want to create loyalty with the Butterfly Customer, the traditional objectives of your media—to create traffic, consumer recognition, and interest—must be changed to a new objective:

To prepare customers to expect the experience they will receive.

Although this shift in perspective may seem slight, it requires a major change in how companies create and analyse their media dimension. Instead of coming up with a campaign and sending it simultaneously to customers and staff, you must first take the steps to ensure you are creating a genuinely attractive offer.

Guarding against creating a fatal attraction is a continuous process of listening to customers, talking to staff, watching behaviour, and testing your own notions against the expectations of your desired customers. So the next time someone brings you a new campaign, or you are in the middle of a marathon agency review, here are some questions to ask yourself to ensure you have a campaign which supports the total business strategy.

- How does the campaign contribute to the communication of your selling proposition and fit with the overall corporate strategy?

- Have we listened to customers and staff sufficiently to know what current beliefs, needs, wants, and emotions we should take into consideration when designing the message?

- What are the benefits to each of the three key stakeholders and how will we know we have achieved them?

- What is the worst thing that could happen and what effect would that have on the three stakeholders?

- What measurements will we use to determine success?

To ensure there is no gap between the tactics and the campaign goal, ask:

- What tactics will work best to help us meet the goal of the campaign?

To ensure an involved and committed team, ask:

- Are all parties involved in the execution at every level aware of the strategy, implementation, delivery, and measurement techniques?
- Are there any barriers to successful implementation (e.g., other priorities, competitive activity, lack of staff or hours, inappropriate design, etc.)?
- What could be the effect on customers and staff if this endeavour were wildly successful?

To ensure a 3-D match, ask:

- What steps have been taken to ensure a match in the physical dimension?
- What proof do we have that the people dimension has sufficient skill and knowledge to interpret the messages accurately?

And to make sure you only ever get better, ask yourself:

- How will we ensure we learn from this investment and avoid repetitive mistakes?

Like Judy George at Domain who refused to allow a media campaign to run because she wasn't sure the staff and the stores could meet the customer's expectations, only go to press when you are sure you can deliver that which you have prepared the customer to expect.

In the next chapter we are going to move into the physical dimension where, once again, it is only a total, integrated approach which protects your trust account with the Monarch Customer.

CHAPTER TEN

The Physical Dimension

THE EMPEROR'S NEW CLOTHES

*After many weeks of experimenting under the sycophantic
eyes of designers and courtiers, the vain emperor was at last
ready to reveal the splendor of his new wardrobe to an
eagerly awaiting crowd. As he stepped onto the balcony
his appearance was greeted by a collective gasp, followed
by a stunned silence until a single, small voice exclaimed,
"But Mother! He's wearing no clothes!"*

Adapted from: *The Emperor and His Clothes, A Fairy Tale*

THE SINGLE SMALL voice in the service sector is that of the Butterfly Customer who quietly echoes the words of the child as they experience modern-day equivalents of the emperor strut about the service parade in glittering, expensive nothings. All too often the emperor's new clothes have little, or no appeal for customers but they don't speak up, they just flit away.

In a search for value in a complex, expensive world, Butterfly Customers are finely attuned to how a company spends its dollars to dress up services or products. They are very aware that every dollar you spend on your premises, physical presence, or other outward packaging is a dollar you can't pass along to them in savings or extra service.

What about you? Haven't you passed the time waiting for your lawyer, doctor, or dentist taking inventory of the works of art on the walls and the opulent surroundings you know you have paid for? Before investing in your external coverings you have to remember there is a crowd standing just outside your balcony waiting to judge whether your choice of apparel is just right, or like that of the emperor, little better than nothing.

The most common gap in the physical dimension is that the company has neglected to get down off the balcony and take a look at the view from below. Here is what you need to do if you want to experience the view through the eyes of the crowd.

1. *Test the Associations.* You must anticipate what the subconscious of your customer will say as they taste, touch, see, and smell the physical dimensions of your business. You can choose what you want your customers to associate you with.

2. *Live in the Customers Shoes.* While many claim to do this, fewer actually succeed. Companies whose physical aspects work and which are in harmony with the other two dimensions *Make the User Chief Designer* and then *Reduce the Frustrations of Change.* And of course, they always *Live up to 3-D Expectations.*

3. *Pass the Real World Test.* In the service sector, the physical dimension is put to hard use by customers and staff, while being expected to last long enough to meet the shareholders return on investment requirements. To meet these standards, companies must pass the real world test.

TEST THE ASSOCIATIONS

Just as the chaos of competition and the economic environment in the customer's external world influence their expectations, the patterns formed in their internal world influence the way in which they view your offering. In the physical dimension, as in every other, you must delve beneath the surface to the subconscious dialogue of the customer to assess their reaction to what you had planned to deliver.

Each tangible aspect of your business has the potential to elicit a wide range of associations from the well-travelled Butterfly Customer. To understand how great companies use this subconscious association in their designs, answer the following questions:

- Why are chefs' garments white?
- Why are the warmers and kitchen counters at McDonald's made of stainless steel?

In our service seminar work, 82% of participants respond with variations on the themes "easier to keep clean" and "sterile." But what are the facts?

Anyone who has tried to cook in a white uniform or get fingerprints off those stainless steel counters knows that neither is easy to keep clean or germfree. But neither fact nor logic will overcome the associations of cleanliness made in the mind of the customer by a pristine white chef's apron and a gleaming stainless steel counter. These associations send such powerful images to the customer's subconscious that we won't see restaurants abandoning these practices anytime soon.

Checking the Subconscious Message

How do you test the associations your customers might have with the various aspects of your physical dimension? Here is how one client succeeded. Faced with lower-than-expected sales of a new line of products the brand manager checked the facts. The expensive in-store display made the products look very good and a competitive shop confirmed that the price was excellent value for the customer. So why wasn't the inventory flying out of the stores? We found the answer in some surprising associations.

Customers in a focus group were asked to evaluate a replica of the display and then tell the moderator what words they associated with the product. They used words like Tiffany, Porsche, and sleek and expensive, hardly what the brand manager had in mind for this "excellent quality for the price" product.

Having uncovered some word associations in a focus group we went to see what we could learn in the store. We watched the customers wander over to the display, stop and look, and leave. When we asked them what they were thinking during their time in the store, they told us:

"This is a very nice store. Look at the beautiful display. Those products look interesting, but I bet they're expensive. No price tags. They must really be expensive."

At this point, a full 40% of customers had convinced themselves they couldn't afford the product and walked away, leaving slightly more than half the potential customer base to build up the nerve to pick up the product and discover that it was not only affordable, but great value for the money!

Customers were associating "no price tags" with jewellery shopping where, they told us, the more expensive the merchandise, the less likely it was to be tagged. The answer for this client was simply to change their display tactics. Prices were featured right on the display where consumers could see them from a distance. Sales rose appreciably the very next month.

Test the associations suggested by your design, package, or product. Use words and pictures to draw out the analogies which are being used by your customer. Because this is one area where nationality and culture can play a huge role, we recommend you hire a specialist if you need to explore the responses of different cultural groups.

Negative Associations

In addition to associations that may inadvertently arise from the customers' experience, there are ones a company creates for itself. And these associations can be negative indeed when the company spends money on "the trappings" of the business. You know, those elements which seem designed for the owner's comfort, pride, or ego rather than for the customer's benefit. What happens where there is a negative association on the part of the customer to the dollars you spend on external trappings and the value to them?

Imagine yourself in 1992. Three years of dismal economic performance have translated into personal pain for millions of people. But throughout this period of doom and gloom, there is one institution which remains unaffected—banks. It seems not to matter how little money there is, it must still flow through banks' fingers, more than a little sticking along the way.

One victim of the economic times was an exclusive spa situated just north of Canada's largest city. Anyone who read the newspapers or watched the news of its demise on TV (and remember Butterfly Customers are well-informed) would have remembered the opulent splendour of the grounds and the magnificence of the internal appointments from the highly publicized opening a few years earlier. But luxury spas, so much in demand in the '80s, were seen as excess in these tough times, and now darkened, this edifice waited for a new owner worthy of the luxury and with deep enough pockets to support the extras. Guess who had enough money?

Right! The mortgage-holding bank, which announced with appropriate fanfare that it was taking over the facility to turn it into a corporate training centre because it had been listening to customers and knew it must invest in training staff to provide better service.

Now, we happened to be doing some research at the time for a major utility on the issue of what type of building a utility needed. In six of the eight focus groups held that week, we heard unprompted comments about the bank plans delivered in a sneering, what-else-can-you-expect-from-these-guys tone. The depth and passion of the response would have astonished those banks' executives who genuinely believed they were making an investment that would be of value to their employees and ultimately benefit customers.

But, customers saw the investment as just one more act of arrogance, ensuring their banking service fees wouldn't drop anytime soon. The image of corporate executives ensconced in marble steam rooms, while fewer and fewer bank tellers struggled to serve customers, was a powerful, negative association.

How Can You Avoid Negative Associations?

It is very difficult not to fall under the charm of the sycophantic vendors. The architect is so convincing, the design house loves the concept, and in the focus groups *they* conducted, customers appear to agree. But that's because they fall back on the old focus group model of asking participants which design they prefer and inviting them to offer their suggestions for what the building should look like. But, dig down deeper and you will hear the sceptical Butterfly Customer's constant questions. *"How much will this cost?" "Why does it have to be so fancy?" "It's beautiful but what does it do?"* or *"It's beautiful but the old one was OK too."*

From ostentatious head offices, to the owner's Mercedes parked in the spot closest to the door to the Persian carpet in the board room, customers perceive that all that glitters is not gold when it comes to the trappings of the business. Before you take that expensive leap into the land of renew, redo, and renovate, test the associations of all the stakeholders and you may be surprised by negative ones. The following factors should be taken into account before spending any significant amount of money on any physical premises:

- First, what is the emotional state of the customer? Take your lead from the economic environment in which your customer is living. Is the economy in good shape or are your customers watching every penny? Is it a time of risk and adventure or are customers hunkering down, making do, and favouring the stability of the tried and true? If the latter is the environment you face, think twice about changing your layout or location.

- What about your staff? A recent survey on employee morale showed one client that the number one concern in the field organization was low pay. This led the client to rethink their store redesign program, and develop a strategy to include employees in the design. Employees will also be included in the creation of the internal communications package to explain to staff the need for the expenditure and how it will contribute to the success of the company. This company knows that it's hard to convince employees you value them if your money is going into trappings instead of looking after their basic needs.

- And, what about the shareholder? They have to look at this decision in light of some results which are very difficult to measure. What effect could employees have if they feel better (or worse) about the new environment? What would happen if the customers viewed the expenditure negatively? Can you really justify the renovation in terms of planned increases in sales or profit? In this era of shrinking margins and precarious profit, it really does take a huge leap of faith to invest hard-won profit into physical surroundings.

- And finally, before one dollar is spent, do an analysis to determine how much greater the benefit could be to you and all your stakeholders if you spent the money on informing, training, developing, and rewarding staff instead.

Techniques to Test the Associations

Traditionally, the public spaces of utilities are designed to send a message of safety and security and reinforce the notion that a single-service provider is best for all concerned. Just think of the post office or train station of yore, where vaulted ceilings and golden wickets put the customer in their place.

But monopolistic organizations in everything from cable TV to gas and public transportation are rapidly being overtaken by free-market competition. Nowhere has this evolution been more evident than in the telephone industry where reduced regulation has led to increased competition. They can no longer rely on "captive" customers, and must learn to think like entrepreneurs who deal daily with Butterfly Customers.

Many telephone companies decided to create a retail front line with "phone stores" located in malls and other places to make it easier for customers to make contact with the company. But, designing these stores to create positive associations in the minds of the customers and avoid the traps of traditional utility design required close listening to the subconscious of the customer.

Here is what focus group customers said about several proposed store designs of a telephone company which wanted to establish a strong retail image.

"So that's where my long distance fees are going!" exclaimed one as a shot of silken wood floors and brass fixtures came up on the screen.

"They'd better not forget to put in the take-a-number-for-service system," muttered another during the slide of a gleaming, marble service counter.

"Well, at least the phones look as expensive as they are," was the opinion of a third as an attractive display unit featuring gleaming equipment flashed on the screen.

What were these customers talking about? What subconscious associations or dialogues were being revealed? We uncovered the following customer beliefs. First, if the company could lower long distance fees when competition arrived, they must have had too much money in the first place, especially when they could build such "expensive" stores. Second, the company could talk all it liked about service, but the nine-to-five mentality would still result in the customer having to wait to be served at the pleasure of the company. Third, the company would never be a good value retailer and the best product deals would be found elsewhere.

When the subconscious of the customer speaks, the emperor (or his CEO) had better listen, before they make an embarrassing balcony appearance. Fortunately, in this case, they were. The early regal designs which suited the era when the phone company was a regulated icon were relegated to the dustbin in favour of a friendlier, simpler look. Later focus groups affirmed that this time the company had it right—the final design delivered the message that this was a company focused on efficiency and good value, and one that values each and every dollar long after it has left the consumer's hand.

Having tested and understood the associations, you're ready to make sure that you have lived in the customer's shoes.

LIVE IN THE CUSTOMER'S SHOES

Considering the amount of money invested in the physical dimension, it is amazing how often the result receives mixed reviews from staff and customers. All too often, the spacious store layout forces customers to waste time, the efficient new head office is farther away, and the new equipment results in lost productivity. This is not what the user would have designed, had they been in charge.

If I Had Been the Chief Designer...

Many cancer-treatment facilities across the continent were designed for a time when the patient load was smaller and personal attention was less costly to provide. The Princess Margaret Hospital in Toronto, recognized as one of the finest and busiest cancer treatment centres in the world, was no exception. Nooks and crannies, intimate, crowded waiting rooms, dowdy surroundings, and insufficient light and space had become a burden as patient loads grew and staff complements shrank. Thousands of outpatients in daily clinics sat in rows of straight-backed chairs lined up around the walls and in every available space right up to the doors of the various clinics.

The announcement of a long-awaited new location was much anticipated by patients and staff alike. Expectations centred around "enough space to serve everyone" and "less time wasted in providing the service." Imagine the initial delight on opening day as all walked into a huge open setting, where a five-storey atrium bathed the balconied floors with sun and warmth.

But the delight quickly became disappointment when the aesthetically pleasing atrium offered little practical benefit. "There's a lot of wasted space here, isn't there?" was the most common refrain from patients who, despite new carpet, paint, and fixtures, felt somehow "removed." And the expected efficiency was never realized as staff now had to escort patients to distant waiting rooms.

Maybe the executive offices are fancier, the research labs better equipped, and the inpatient care section bigger, but these aspects of the building are seen by a relative few. The real face of the business (and that's what it is) is the one seen by the multitude of patients and friends who experience daily this new, but less efficient, presentation. Their comments? *"It's nice but it doesn't have the comfortable feeling of the old place." "This is so unfair for the staff,"* said one elderly lady. *"They work so hard as it is and now they have to walk hundreds of extra miles a week."*

The designer of the new building *had* consulted with staff and patients, asking them what they wanted from the redesigned space. So what happened? What is the difference between seeking input and making the user the chief designer?

Make the User the Chief Designer

You make the user the chief designer by integrating the expertise of the professionals with the experience of the user. This means making sure the designer has the ability to experience their designs just as a user would. They must be able to set aside what they know about aesthetics, architecture, and building codes and act like an ordinary user would.

Ben Barkow, a Toronto psychologist, has spent several decades trying to persuade the designers of massive public spaces to get down from their lofty perchs and walk through the implications of their designs. Anyone who has stood in the washroom line-up at intermission in a stadium or auditorium knows how many more designers need to take his advice.

His words of wisdom aren't just about major projects. From designing the interior of the airplane, or a teller's wicket, to deciding where to put the cash desk in the boutique, companies that live in the shoes of the customer and staff deliver the amenities and productivity both crave. Here are some ways to get your design team down from their perch.

Read the Emotional Flow, Not Just the Traffic Flow

In design, one key issue is always traffic flow. The business asks the designer questions such as: How do we get customers from A to B efficiently? How do we encourage them to spend more time in our building to see the variety of services we are offering? The measure of success is a space which provides a good flow, yet encourages people to linger. But the designer who neglects to take the time to read customer emotions as they experience that flow may unwittingly add to Butterfly behaviour.

The IKEA catalogue and ads lead you to expect a functional store design. Simplicity and practicality are at the heart of their message, and wasted energy would not be part of the IKEA concept. Right? Wrong! On an assignment to return some merchandise, we were amazed at the length of time it took.

Shoppers had expected that the return would be quick and easy, but their initial delight in seeing the return/cash area close to the entrance quickly turned to dismay. As they followed the signs through a meandering pathway up and down and through what felt like (and in fact was) the entire store, they realized that the store design was forcing them to take a detour. Rather than inciting them to buy more, this roundabout path just made them angry and determined not to return.

IKEA listened and fixed the problem. Now stores provide a well-marked "straight-in" entrance for the customer burdened with an item to return.

When your design team unveils the traffic patterns and pathways, ask them how customers are going to be feeling as they make their way through the premises. If they don't know, send them to find out. The use of virtual reality in design is paving the way in allowing customers to "experience" the design before a single nail is hammered, but until that technology is available to us all, behavioural observations and exit interviews are an excellent way to do this. Go and observe customers using your existing facility, as well as locations similar to the one you are planning.

Anticipate the Effect in the Hands of the Staff

One client wanted to encourage greater face-to-face contact with the customer. Instead of personnel stationed behind counters, the new design was meant to encourage staff to be out serving customers. But once the design was put into effect, staff continued to wait behind the counter for customers to approach. What had the designer missed?

The store design, with its attractive merchandising and hands-on displays, encouraged customers to browse and wander. The customers, motivated by the new design were touching displays, moving inventory, and taking products off the shelves. It was taking the staff twice as long to clean up the displays as it had before, with no additional help. Staff felt they had to leave someone "on duty" behind the counter so other team members could do the required tidying up. Customers, seeing a person stationed behind a service counter went there for help, instead of to one of the "busy" workers on the floor.

The designer needed to think through how the design would affect the behaviour of customers and staff, either adding more personnel, or adjusting the design accordingly.

One way to avoid such problems is to have the staff take a look at the designs or work with the 3-D computer model to tell you how they feel it would affect their daily routine. Many frontline staff have worked in a variety of service environments and may have some insightful comments about what could happen in the new situation.

Making the user the chief designer is not just about asking customers and staff what they want. It is about learning how the customers would like to experience your offering and then letting the designers apply their professional skills to deliver it. Designers must take responsibility for understanding exactly how the proposed design is going to feel to customers and what it will be like to work in for staff.

Reduce the Frustrations of Change

A new design or new package is about change. The company that wants to protect its trust account balance with the Butterfly Customer always anticipates the effect of that change. How will it affect the customer?

One client had the jarring experience of receiving an award for his new store design one week and attending a customer focus group the next. Instead of the expected accolades, customers said: *"Every time I go there, what I want is in a different place." "The new signs were great. Too bad the merchandise was never located where the sign pointed."* The client was first surprised and then horrified, but his staff weren't. They already knew because they had spent a significant amount of time since the redesign providing directions, explanations, and listening to customers grousing.

We are constantly bemused as owners, designers, and management "tour" each new or renovated facility congratulating each other on the great job they have done in the physical dimension, while confused customers wander in their wake.

Grocery stores are perhaps the masters in the art of retail prestidigitation: "Now you see it, now you don't." Just stay away from your favourite grocery store for a month or two and then walk directly to aisle three and put your hand on the top shelf and find your favourite product has disappeared. Your initial surprise (remember that Uh-oh feeling!) is followed by increasing frustration as you attempt to find someone who can direct you to the needed product. This escalates as you then find that many other favourites have also taken a walk since you were last in the store. Grocery shopping is an activity many consumers like to complete while on automatic pilot, so while there may be momentary increases in sales from shifts in merchandise, there is also a corresponding increase in Butterfly behaviour.

The change merry-go-round increases consumer discomfort as they are never quite sure who you are or how to interact with you. Customers pay in wasted time and staff pay by answering endless questions about where to find things and how much something really costs. But change is a way of life, especially in the competitive retail and service sectors. How do you reduce the frustrations for customers? Let us look at two areas, changing environments and changing prices.

Changing Environments

When customers visit you often, how do you provide them with a varying experience without causing frustration? The retail world addresses this opportunity by remerchandising the store and redoing the displays. The IKEA Marketing Outpost was one clever approach that had a brief life in midtown Manhattan in 1995-96.

This successful home-furnishings staple of the suburbs, knew it was a physical mismatch to try to recreate its sprawling environs in downtown Manhattan. Yet, when an opportunity arose, IKEA jumped at the chance of having a presence on these high traffic streets. The result was a 7,500 sq. ft. space at 53rd and Lexington, designed to take a theme and run it in short, six-week cycles. Concepts such as IKEA Cooks, IKEA Plays, and IKEA Sleeps, each called for a total redo of the store.

How did the chain keep up this frantic pace without causing a moment's frustration for customers or staff? Staff product specialists from other stores were brought in to provide information for both customers and staff. This is change that worked. Customers received the best in product knowledge and staff had the support of experts, and the fun of working in midtown. Information about each change was provided with signs and a newsletter, and the shop even closed down, with plenty of warning, to avoid customers and staff being discombobulated during the change-overs.

Getting staff prepared with the required information on the product or process, keeping staff and customers informed during the change process, and doing the changeover in a way that causes the least inconvenience are the secrets of those companies that are able to change with the least frustration for the Butterfly Customer.

Changing Prices

Consumers and staff alike have been totally confused by constantly changing prices in the retail and service industry. If something has a value of $100 today, how can it be worth $75 for three days of a sale, and then return to a value of $100?

The scepticism surrounds not only the "sale" but most other promotional discounts as well. Just ask any customer who has received a "scratch & save" coupon. This gimmick offers a discount from, say, 10% to 35%; the actual discount is revealed when the customer brings the coupon to the store and makes a purchase. The suspicious Butterfly Customer believes that the majority of the hidden boxes will reveal only the 10% discount and that the entire scheme is misleading. In a time of increasing mistrust, this may be one discount tactic which deserves to be abandoned.

How do you take advantage of the opportunities presented by adjusting your prices and offering exciting discount programs, while minimizing the frustrations that can be felt by your customers?

Make sure you offer a reason for the change in price. Customers understand the concept of promotional buys, seat sales during off-peak travel seasons, end-of-season clearouts. Put the reason in your media dimension and repeat it again in the physical dimension.

Watch very carefully how you change the prices. Using black ink to hide the former price is not a practice designed to build trust. Nor are four different price tags (an experience which is altogether too common). Show the customer the progression of price changes so they can make up their own mind about the value.

Finally, decide how you are going to handle the start and close date of a sale price. If there are strict dates, say so and ensure they are maintained for every customer.

Change is a fact of life, and in the physical dimension you must make sure that you reduce the frustrations from the customer's perspective.

You have made sure the customer was the chief designer, you have taken steps to reduce the frustration of change. The final piece to living in the shoes of the customers is to check the match between the physical and the media and people dimensions.

Live Up To 3-D Expectations

Here is an example of how Northern Reflections has brought financial rewards to its parent F. W. Woolworth throughout North America by delivering consistent harmony in the physical dimension, even as it evolved and changed during three years of explosive growth.

Northern Reflections was inspired by the spirit of cottage country. From its birthplace in Ontario, through evolutions throughout Canada and into the United States, stores perfectly married the promise of a woodsy, back-to-nature store with store guarantees written on logs, through to the Adirondak chairs for in-store seating, beamed ceilings, and store staff dressed in sweatshirts featuring nature scenes and outdoor colours.

Even in later iterations of the store concept for children and men, the chain remained true to its roots as it rolled out over 250 stores in fewer than five years. The team had lived in the shoes of the customer and understood how to integrate the other two dimensions with the physical one.

Living in the shoes of the customer is taking the time and energy to imagine in detail exactly what it is like in your present or future physical dimension. Anticipating the effects in advance can help you bring a strong physical presence to market.

Pass the Real World Test

Every investment in the physical dimension must deliver results over a period of time. From the cardboard stand-up display that needs to last through a back-to-school campaign, to an airline terminal designed to survive a decade of hard use, dollars spent on the physical plant, packaging, and fixtures eat profits unless they deliver for the expected period of time. All too often the gap between the fancy display created in a head office workroom and the picked over disaster which greets late Saturday afternoon shoppers is great indeed.

By the early 1990s, it was obvious that Microsoft had created a brand which was recognized by customers. Customers looking for new software were interested in seeing what Microsoft products were available. The company responded to the opportunity by creating in-store kiosks which clustered together a variety of game, productivity, and informational products onto a single Microsoft display stand. They even included restocking reminder cards just like bookstores do.

It was a great idea, but in several stores we visited, the display was listing to the left because the flimsy plastic legs buckled. In others, all customers saw were the out-of-stock reminder cards after merchandise fell off when staff tried to restock the unit.

Microsoft quickly abandoned this unit and has since insisted that materials going to the stores go through a more rigorous testing. Another hint that Microsoft is getting their dimensions in sync is their new in-store displays featuring the same message from their media campaign, as customers are asked "Where do you want to go today?" in the merchandise presentation.

OBJECTIVE: To put your new design through the "crash test."

PROCESS: Create a prototype or mock-up as close to the final proposed product as possible. Wal-Mart has a full-size store in a warehouse where staff can experiment and test layouts, designs, and fixtures.

Ask staff to identify the toughest situations: the first day of a sale, a day when the front line is short-handed, etc. Put the design through its paces, setting up a test on-site or inviting a team to try out the mock-up.

TACTIC: In today's service world, many people work on their own, with limited training or guidance from supervisors. How will the new part-time employee learn to interact with the display, design or equipment? You may need to rewrite the instructions or think about a new training plan to meet the needs of this target audience.

Customers can tell us about hundreds of examples of what were probably once a nice design or an attractive display that had fallen apart in the real world. From black counters that show every speck of dust, to glass shelves which streak, and shelving units that don't adapt to changing products, the physical dimension is filled with examples of designs that don't work as well as they should.

Create your own version of the crash test dummies used in the auto industry and test your design to ensure that it will deliver in the real world.

CLOSING THE GAP IN THE PHYSICAL DIMENSION

Before you commit cash to a fixed asset with which you and your customers will have to live, your design team had better have very clear evidence that they have taken the following issues into account.

1. Test the Associations:

> How has the design team determined how your customer will feel about this design? What research was done?

> When was the research done? Before or after the design was complete? Were customer and staff comments and feelings taken into account in the creation of the design?

> What message does it send about your corporate values? Will customers, staff, or shareholders find you "trapped in the trappings?"

2. Live in the Customer's Shoes:

> How will this design enhance employee productivity and the customer experience?

> Are staff and customers in agreement about how the design will increase their productivity and the customer experience?

3. Pass the Real World Test:

How will this design work in the most remote location with the newest employee?

How will this work for the customer and staff two weeks, six months, or a year from now?

In the media dimension you have ensured that you have an attractive offer and not a fatal attraction. Following these steps in the physical dimension will ensure that your balcony appearance will be greeted by genuine admiration. And now, it is time to tackle the people dimension.

The People Dimension

W HILE A MISMATCH between the first two dimensions can cause Uh-oh feelings and the ensuing erosion of trust, it does not produce the emotional heat we find when the disharmony occurs in the people dimension. As your customer experiences the media and physical dimension of your business, they develop (and then adjust) their expectations of the delivery relatively easily. Your people dimension represents the biggest opportunity to turn Butterfly into Monarch, or vice versa.

This dimension, where programs, gimmicks, and impossible service objectives were designed for the front-line staff in attempts to garner customer loyalty, succeeds too often only in creating more Butterflies.

So just what are the attributes of the people dimension in a service or retail company that Monarch Customers love to trust? How would one describe the perfect people dimension? Well, the description is not the traditional one so beloved of service and training gurus—employees who cheerfully serve all and never hesitate to run a mile to satisfy a single customer.

It is rather:

- employees who *add value* to the experience for the maximum number of customers on a consistent basis.

Value implies that you get what you paid for, and *value added*, that you got more than you paid for. How does this price-related notion translate into the people dimension? The articulate, knowledgeable Butterfly Customer knows that included in the price of the goods or service are the wages you pay your people. If there is no added value from this additional cost then the customer, rightly, will ask, "What am I paying for anyway?"

The Butterfly's answer to this is, "Nothing much," which explains much of the last decade's shift away from full-price, full-service operations to discounters with lower levels of service, and the current rush to self-serve, such as Internet commerce.

LESSONS FROM THE PRICE WARS

One of the great conundrums in the service industry over the last decade has been the variance between what customers say they value in the people dimension (expensive, personal service) and what is delivered in the businesses they actually patronize (the lowest price and limited staff).

Certainly, if you follow much of the reported consumer behaviour, you would come away convinced customers will always migrate to lower prices. After all, the dramatic shift in market share from full-service department stores to discounters such as Wal-Mart is proof positive. Or is it?

In 1992, the exchange rate and differences in retail practices had resulted in a "price gap" between Canadian stores and those just across the border. We did a telephone survey of 500 cross-border shoppers, and expected a very high proportion to cite lower prices as their primary reason for making the trip to the United States.

Surprise, surprise. Only half of the 500 shoppers interviewed named price as their primary motivation; 20% said it was for a better assortment or the shopping environment itself. The remaining 30% said it was the higher level of service they received south of the 49th parallel that drew their dollars away from Canadian retailers.

That's not all. When we asked for secondary reasons for travelling to shop, a full 60% talked about service. All told, 90% of our survey respondents mentioned service as either a primary or secondary reason for shopping in the United States.

In follow-up questions these customers talked about the fact that what drew them back to the United States was the extra service they received, and at a lower price. The Canadian merchants weren't even in the game when it came to an overall value-added experience.

ARE YOUR EMPLOYEES ADDING VALUE?

Business must explore the question "Are our employees adding value to the customer interaction?" The answer is "no" if they are tied up fixing disharmony caused by a mismatch among the other dimensions or mistakes caused by your business practices. In fact, superhuman service, sporadically delivered, may do more to decrease trust, as customers approach each interaction with trepidation, unsure what they will receive this time.

The most common gap in the people dimension is that there is no value added for customers that would cause them to want to return or refer others to you. When we find this gap, we direct clients to answer two questions.

Have you selected the right service strategy? The service you promise must actually reflect what customers really value when doing business with you. You must also explore if can you afford to deliver it consistently.

Are employees able to add value? Employees who are busy with other dimensions of the business are not available to serve customers and have no time to add value. In fact, many tell us that they barely have enough time to do the basic job. What are the practices of your business that interfere with employees' ability to focus on delivering the service strategy? Before you even think about creating an expectation in which staff are to add extra value, make sure you have concrete evidence that they are currently meeting basic expectations.

SELECT THE RIGHT SERVICE STRATEGY

To ensure the people dimension contributes to a holistic, harmonious experience, one of the questions you have to decide is just what level of service is appropriate for your customers. For instance, if you own a shoe store, is it best to pile the boxes on the floor and let customers take care of their own needs, or is your selling proposition better served through sales associates providing on-their-knees service?

The key is to select a service strategy which you can afford to deliver consistently, and match it to your strategy, your customer's expectations contract, your media campaigns, and your physical presence.

Here are the three broad options you have to work with.

1. Full Service
2. Service When I Ask for It
3. Self Service

Full Service

Once upon a time, full service was the standard by which all service was measured. Full service is the personal attention given by an attentive service provider devoted to helping a customer through the interaction with the business. The recent purging of staff in an attempt to cut costs, combined with the emergence of the Butterfly Customer has resulted in an environment where full service is the exception, rather than the rule. It's a level of service that almost no one provides but almost everyone aspires to. But is it the right service level for your customer and how do you decide whether full service is the right strategy for your business? Here are a series of questions we find useful.

- Who are the market leaders in my price level and what are they doing in the people dimension of the business?

  Look at other companies (not just direct competition) and see what they are doing to add value for the customer. What level of product knowledge do they have? What is the staff to customer ratio and how long do customers have to wait for personal attention? What activities are staff doing to exceed customer expectations? Do they deliver the finished suit to the customer's office, or complete the computer set-up in the purchaser's home?

  But be careful because this is the point where too many companies go off the rails. They take a look at the competition and then run back to implement those ideas in their own organization. Before rushing off in all directions, take the time to answer three more critical questions.

- Will doing this have a positive effect on the relationship between my staff and the customers and ultimately with me?

  Make sure that these extras really do add value in the eyes of the customer. Conduct some focus groups with the customers of those "best practices" organizations and explore whether the actions you are considering are creating Monarchs, or just Butterflies who are taking a little rest.

- How much will it cost?

    Offering full service is expensive. It takes a concerted effort to bring staff to peak operating levels and keep them there. Companies such as Disney spend a fortune to select, train, and develop the people dimension in their theme parks. They know it is worth it to them but is it really worth it for your customers, your staff, and your shareholders?

TIP

OBJECTIVE: To check the real cost of full-service delivery.

PROCESS: Create a list of the knowledge and skills employees should have, for instance, what level of product knowledge, what complexity of transactions, what ability to communicate, etc.

Estimate the costs per employee of reaching that level, compared to your present standard. This includes training, recruiting, and salary premiums. And, don't forget the added management time required to manage people who are building relationships and not just completing forms or doing paperwork.

Test your current team and see how close they are to the revised expectations. What would it cost to keep everyone at the desired level all the time?

Take a look at your staffing patterns and ask: What would the extra cost be of ensuring customers are always able to receive this level of service within a reasonable time?

TACTIC: Have your human resources department cost out a certification program in which formal training and assessment guarantees a certain proficiency. See how much it will cost per employee in training fees and extra staffing. Don't start down this road unless you are sure there is a pay-off for customers, staff, and shareholders.

- Will it be sustainable?

The saddest situation of all for customers, staff, and shareholders alike is when an organization rushes to increase its service to full-service standards but just as quickly falls back to the old service model when times get tough. You must make certain you are really prepared to commit yourself to a certain level of quality and volume of staff, no matter what.

Full service will never disappear completely as a service strategy, but it is on the decline not only due to cost cutting but to changing customer preferences as well. If you decide it is right for you, here is an example of one company that delivers it very well indeed.

A Full-Service Promise, Value-Added Delivery

Lenscrafters Optical is an operation which clearly signals the full-service promise in its media and physical dimensions, and then delivers in the people dimension.

Since glasses are a purchase consumers cannot complete on their own, staff expertise and personal attention can only help the customer feel more comfortable as they work to arrive at the right decision. Lenscrafters creates this expectation in the customer's mind in television and print ads featuring a one-to-one interaction between a staff member and customer, where the customer is receiving something of value. Customers are portrayed having their glasses fitted properly, or receiving advice. In the physical dimension, the store design features workstations where the optician or consultant confers privately with a customer to select and fit the right frames. The design not only encourages the one-to-one relationship, it ensures it.

The people dimension is designed to match. Stores are staffed by a combination of opticians and trained fashion consultants in sufficient numbers to provide individual attention. It is their job not only to "sell" a pair of eyeglasses but create a lasting relationship with a customer who will feel they got "more" than they expected.

Only elect the full-service model if it adds value in the eyes of the customer and you can afford to provide it to all. Because it is the most labor-intensive service model many companies are currently rethinking its appropriateness.

Service When I Ask for It

This is the most prevalent service model today. It acknowledges that customers rarely get through the entire experience without requiring some kind of direct interaction with the people dimension, but that customers may be quite happy to do most of the work themselves. It could be the Butterfly seeking to be "in control" by doing more of the fact finding and decision making, or a customer who believes that a little extra work on their part gains them some savings in price or time.

In this model, staff are expected to be available as needed to complete specific tasks, provide assistance in locating items, accepting returns, filling out forms, etc. A vast number of service providers and retailers work on this "cafeteria" model. The customer must initiate the contact or request and staff are supposed to respond with the answer or solution. No more, no less.

The trick to this model is that when customers decide they want service, they want it immediately. The challenge is to be sure staff are available to provide service when the customer asks for it. Here are the questions we ask clients to help them evaluate the effectiveness of their "service when I ask for it" model.

- Have you evaluated how you compare to other similar operations that do a good job of having the customer do most of the work?

Go beyond the direct competitors to other industries or sectors. Look for operations that run with fewer staff than the industry average and yet have a reputation with customers for excellent service. What are they doing to create this sense of service?

• Have you observed sufficient numbers of customers experiencing the service in your company to be able to confidently identify the points where they need or want service?

In addition to the obvious points of payment and returns, look for times when the customer might be aided by information or advice. Then, look at the physical dimension and seek opportunities to deliver the service customers are looking for through signage or layout. U.S. discounter Target put information telephones throughout the store so customers could call for information and assistance.

• Does the staff level reflect the service promise?

In a "service when I ask for it" environment, one of the first things customers do is to check that there will be staff available if needed. They are reassured by the sight of people who look as if they are serving customers, or could be. When they see staff hunkered down, avoiding eye contact at all costs, they know it will be difficult to get the service you promised.

Staff to customer ratio is an important measure in both full service and service when I ask for it. Clients are often confused when we ask them to give us the number of staff "available to serve the customer" in a certain hour and not the number of staff on the schedule. It's not the same thing. Knowing how many staff have been truly available is key to being able to evaluate which level of service you want to, and can, provide.

TIP

> **OBJECTIVE:** To learn whether staff are available to deliver "service when the customer asks for it."
>
> **PROCESS:** Do a payroll analysis to find out how many staff were scheduled during a fairly busy period.
>
> Next, do an analysis of what duties the staff were expected to complete in this period. Restocking, tabulating, completing paperwork, preparing reports, and responding to requests, are all examples of work that may keep the staff person on the schedule but unavailable to serve.
>
> Use behavioural observations to check what demands customers typically place on the staff during the same period of time.
>
> Don't forget to account for meals and personal breaks.
>
> **TACTIC:** Observe the staff to see what defensive behaviour they use. Do they work with their heads down or turned away from the customer so they won't "see" people waiting to be served?

Creating a Service Atmosphere

One company which has done an excellent job of giving the customer just the level of service they want, while keeping payroll at an affordable level, is Eddie Bauer, the Seattle-based retailer. Here, staff interaction is a matter of course whether the customer is buying $5 socks or a $500 down-filled parka. Unlike Lenscrafters where there *has* to be a full service, one on one contact model for the actual purchase, Eddie Bauer operates in a market where a customer could easily do the work with little or no contact with the people dimension. They could make a purchase from a catalogue, a discount outlet, or even on the Internet, and yet they flock to the store. Why? Because the company consistently puts the customer first and clearly demonstrates a willingness on the part of the staff to "serve" the customer.

We regularly send our mystery customers out to key service providers and retailers to provide benchmarks for our clients, and Eddie Bauer is consistently in the top 10% across North America. What are staff doing that puts them in this category? "Heads-up" is the order of the day. Staff seem tuned to always know where customers are, and are ready to anticipate their needs, regardless of what operational work is being done. Yes, the store gets stocked, the paperwork completed, and payroll costs are within industry guidelines, but the customer gets value-added service when they ask for it.

In the service sector, payroll is often the largest ongoing expense so certainly a "service when I ask" model appears to be more financially rewarding in today's highly competitive environment. The challenge for you is to design your physical dimension and operational model so that it takes only limited number of staff to offer service when the customer wants it.

Self Service

True self service allows the customer to complete the transaction with no direct contact with any human being. Technology has replaced what people used to do—take cash, answer questions, or provide information. The contract between you and your customer implies agreement that assistance from the people dimension will be offered as an exception, rather than as a rule. Vending machines, automated teller machines (ATMs), and the Internet are all examples of reducing the people dimension as close to zero as possible.

The high costs associated with the people dimension are causing retailers and service providers to find a way to do the deal or conclude the transaction without any human contact. How well does this trend suit the Butterfly Customer who yearns to be a Monarch? Isn't that desirable creature almost always attracted to a service experience with at least an element of the people dimension about it? How do you take advantage of the self-serve trend and still build trust with your customers?

If you are moving into a truly self-serve environment from a fuller service one, the most dangerous time is during the transition. Before embarking on this activity, you must determine some things in advance.

- How familiar are your customers with any technology you would use to replace staff?

  The pioneers in self-serve technology have paid part of the price for you to take advantage of a new system. They have introduced many consumers to new ways of doing business. However, it is possible that your customer has no familiarity with, or interest in, allowing technology to take the place of a human in the interaction. Some research will help you determine where your customers are in the technology race. Take a tip from the catalogue companies and make certain you provide sufficient information to allow even the most technologically-illiterate customer to easily and successfully complete the transaction.

- Are you willing to lose personal contact with your customer?

  If you implement a self-service strategy, you lose the interpretive ability of the front-line staff. You may say the staff don't do any interpretation of customer likes, dislikes, wants, or needs. Maybe, but best to be sure before you abandon the other service levels. Remember, one of the traits of loyal customers is that they give you information about your competition and make suggestions for your business.

OBJECTIVE: To determine what market intelligence front-line staff provide.

PROCESS: Track the source of your decision-making information to determine just how much of it comes from the front line. Find out if VPs go out and talk to staff. Do buyers, merchandisers, or product developers talk to staff? Do staff offer suggestions that go up the line and end up influencing executive decisions?

TACTIC: Just to keep your research honest, survey the staff and ask them to list two pieces of advice or valuable business information they have given to their manager or the company in the past twelve months.

When moving to a self-serve model you should take extra care in designing the information flow and processes to be able to still capture customer input. This may range from installing "video interview booths" which allow the customer to talk to you via camera, to a measurement system which records how long it takes a customer to complete a transaction.

You're On Your Way

One example of self service, is the automated service station, where the customer is led through a truly self-serve experience with prompts and signs. Staff only appear in the event of an emergency. The media promise "You're on your way with Esso" is matched by the site's well-lit machines with big type and instructions in plain language. A credit card inserted into the pump and a four-digit transaction number keyed into a pad at the car wash, and the customer has initiated and completed the total transaction without the aid of the people dimension.

This will be the service category with the explosive growth in the coming decades, just as service when I ask for it was in the last. Delivering it requires you to understand exactly what customers will want without the benefit of having the interpretive skills of front-line employees.

Mix and Match Service Strategies

Beyond the three broad classifications, many companies are fine-tuning their strategy on a department by department basis. Remember that educated Butterfly Customer? They don't need or want to pay for value-added service when they pick a can of shaving cream off the shelf, but they will be annoyed if there isn't someone (with the appropriate skill and knowledge) available immediately at that new pharmacy counter featured in your ads as a "full-service department."

Take a warehouse retailer for instance. Whether it is Sam's Club in Austin, Texas, Hypermarche in Dijon, France, or Costco in Seattle, Washington, the customer will be presented with different service options in various sections of the store.

Full service is provided at the optical counter; "service when I ask for it" at the food counter, cash and returns desk; and self service at the automated teller machine. This is not a problem in terms of providing harmony for the customer as long as the signals are clear in the other two dimensions. The modern consumer responds positively to a service provider who matches the "costly" staff complement to the needs of the consumer. They know how much it costs you, and ultimately them, to have extra staff standing around providing no visible value added.

Once the service strategy has been determined and you have ensured it is a match to the promises made in the first two dimensions, it is time to evaluate how the service level you have selected is being delivered,

Staff encumbered by glitches in your systems—by inappropriate processes, inefficient design, and inadequate resources or training—are not able to offer extra value to customers. That is the second question you must ask: Are staff *able* to add value?

ARE YOUR PEOPLE *Able* TO ADD VALUE?

For the most part, people working on the front lines of the service sector would prefer to be working in a way which adds value to customers. The two things they need from you are: a consistent service priority; and the skills to make the impersonal, personal.

A Consistent Service Priority

When service slips out of first place in the priority list, it is often because the shareholder has slipped into sole possession of the controls. In a full-service environment, when sales become the goal instead of the measure, everyone is focused on making the sale, from the barracuda-like salespeople who tackle customers at the entrance to the store, to their managers who start every staff conversation with " Did you close the sale with that customer?"

In the other service environments, this corporate concentration on numbers is likely to translate into a focus on the clerical aspects of the business and running with the leanest possible number of staff.

"If you're not a mat, get up off the floor and serve me"

Customers wonder why all those people wearing nifty uniforms in those big box stores can't even direct store traffic to the right aisle, much less stop gossiping to other staff long enough to respond to a direct customer question.

A recent observation of a customer's attempt to purchase a few items from the deli counter of a supermarket festooned with banners proclaiming "Customer First" provides a clear example. The customer, (soon joined by two others) watched five employees deliberately avoid the eye contact which would have required them to stop what they were doing to provide service to customers who were clearly in need of it. Two managers (so said their badges) worked on a weighing machine, while two staff vacuum-packed deli meats under the eagle eye of a fifth employee. When the customer's direct request for help finally penetrated the consciousness of one of the managers, his look of annoyance at being interrupted was followed by a command to someone else to do the "dirty work" of serving the customer. Why have a deli counter where customers can do none of the work unless staff are told that their *primary* function when behind the counter is to watch for, or better yet, anticipate that customer signal for help?

TIP

OBJECTIVE: Count the real impact of running a business with insufficient staff available to serve the customer.

PROCESS: The next time you are engaged in a discussion about the sales made last month, ask the team: "I wonder how many we lost?"

TACTIC: Install some form of traffic counter that not only records the number of customers who enquire or enter in a given hour but also records the number of staff who were "available" to serve.

The shareholder is best served when staff and customers have a consistent service priority. This means adjustments to payroll hours must be made very carefully and with close attention to the real impact they will have on service. Rather than managing payroll hours, take a look at your staff-to-customer ratio. At what point do you start to lose customers due to insufficient staff? What other things can be done to help customers serve themselves? These are the kind of questions that take care of the shareholder, employee, and customer while maintaining the service priority.

Make the Impersonal, Personal

The people dimension is your opportunity to:

- smooth out the rough edges
- gain information and insight from Monarchs
- conduct ongoing customer research
- adjust the delivery to individual needs.

Employees tied up with chores or in short supply can't offer this added value. Neither can those who lack the skill and insight to make the impersonal experience, personal. Employees who personalize the experience don't act like robots. Rather, they are thinking human beings who constantly adjust their service delivery to suit the situation and the customer.

Nowhere is making the impersonal, personal more critical than in the full-service model. Customers will not report they "got more than they paid for" unless the staff has the skill to "gain permission" from the customer to get an interaction started, offer advice, help with the buying decision and suggest items to meet a range of needs. And yet, establishing a comfort level with the customer in order to gain permission to do these activities can be very difficult indeed.

The Comfort Zone

Imagine yourself at the entrance to a high-fashion men's store, women's boutique, or furniture store watching as the customer enters. "Hi. May I help you?" spoken by a staff person with a friendly smile within the first ten feet of the entrance.

"No thanks, I'm just looking." says the suddenly stiff customer, turning sideways and not even looking the attendant in the eye. And yet less than a minute later, this same customer is muttering under her breath that "service just isn't what it used to be" as she impatiently awaits her turn at the service trough.

Why is there this tension between customer and associate when a full-service provider does what customers have said they want—offer personal attention and service? Because the practice of offering attentive service often conflicts with the customer's need to gain some comfort and control in what may be an unfamiliar space or situation.

Staff should greet instantly, with a nonthreatening person-to-person smile, wave or nod, but they must understand the it is the customer who will give permission to move to a salesperson-customer interchange. Look for a communications or sales program which understands this customer need for comfort and provides skills in increasing that comfort, rather than just closing the sale. The pay-off to you is employees who can create a very personal interpretation of your business to a wide range of customers.

Who Is My Customer Anyway?

Would a billionaire be targeted as a customer of a discount warehouse chain? Newspaper magnate Ken Thomson buys his socks on sale and Sam Walton was always his own best customer. There are numerous stories of the very rich who shopped the same way as those living pay cheque to pay cheque. Income, age, education, and household size have less and less to do with how we think and what we do.

Timothy Leary and George Bush were always closer in age than in values, and the same can be said of Bill Clinton and radio talk show bad boy, Howard Stern. And, GenXer Bill Gates is the same age as all those sales people pushing Windows 95 on the retail selling floor, years after they expected to be applying their university degree in the profession of their choice.

Although your customers may share the same postal code, live in identical houses, have two point five children and earn about the same amount, they may each see the world from an entirely different point of view. They would be insulted if someone said they were the same…and so would we. Yet, every hour of every day, each of us receives the identical offers for products and services and attempts are made to engage us in a contract using a common frame of reference touting the same features and benefits. How does a business meet the challenge of creating a personal experience in a mass media world? It is in the people dimension that the business has the best opportunity to present the product or service in the attractive light of individual needs and wants.

Why Will You Buy?

Although laden with treasure, you are dying of thirst in the desert. Magically, three salespeople appear, each carrying a carafe of clear liquid which can be purchased in exchange for all your gold. Dry-throated, you listen to their pitches:

"After a long walk, I am sure your feet are sore. This product will soothe your toes," cries the first.

"My product will be sure to clean your dusty garment as white as when it was purchased," croons the second.

*"My product will instantly quench your raging thirst," pro-
claims the third sales pro.*

Who gets your gold? No contest in this case. The water salesperson who featured the product benefit which met your most press-
ing need is the winner.

Imagine the power of a staff who understands the needs that
are uppermost in the minds of your customers as they approach
your business. Everyone of us would like our feet to be soothed,
our clothes to be cleaned, our thirst to be quenched after a walk
in the desert. The employee skilled in making the impersonal,
personal can quickly promote the benefits which most closely
align with the needs of your customers.

Personal Service at the Cash

How do staff make the impersonal, personal, in the midst of conducting the chores of the service-when-I-ask world? Here is how
one employee succeeded.

With eight busy cash lines inching forward, a customer found
himself in a line just behind a boy and his cake-box-laden dad.
When the cake box reached the price scanner, the cashier smiled
directly at the young lad. "And is this a birthday cake?" Her
warmth and interest was genuine and earned an eager response,
with lots of details. She created a brief moment of delight as the
child's father beamed and the entire line-up smiled in the pleasure of a small child's anticipation of his afternoon party.

That young woman had succeeded in creating a personal
moment for a half-dozen busy shoppers with one simple question
and a great smile, while rapidly completing the task of process-
ing payment. A quick look up and down the cash desks uncovered a picture where almost every cashier appeared to be
engaged in similar, smiling conversation with the customers.

Let's hope these cashiers are paid well because they are clearly creating a personal moment for nearly every customer they come into contact with.

In evaluating the people dimension, the two key aspects to examine are the appropriateness of the service strategy and how staff are able to add value. One of the most powerful techniques we know to explore these is the use of mystery customers.

TIP

OBJECTIVE: To provide the skills to make the impersonal, personal.

PROCESS: Define the skills needed for your environment. We generally find they are: the skill to increase customer comfort, listening, finding things out, and testing and validating what is being heard.

Seek a program or select a supplier who can help with both these personal skills and also the professional knowledge required. The Butterfly Customer wants someone who has worthwhile information to share.

Ensure the staff know why you are introducing this kind of training—to add value, to get to know customers better, to personalize the experience.

TACTIC: Finding out about the customer is a key skill. Have the staff play "Twenty Questions" imagining all the things they would like to know about their customers. Then, help them turn those questions into ones which won't offend the customer. There are many good question-asking skills-building programs available on the market to provide you and your staff with guidance.

MYSTERY CUSTOMERS

Why not just ask real customers, you say? Certainly you can but the danger with using only customers to learn the details of the experience is short-term memory loss! Think about the last meal you ate out. Now imagine yourself the subject of a research questionnaire. Just how detailed would your memory be? Certainly you could provide an overall rating of the experience. Perhaps you would remember the server and the details of how the meal was presented. But could you tell the researcher how many seconds (or minutes) you waited to be greeted, to be seated, to be served, to be billed? Would you remember the words used by your host and what were all the other staff doing? Could you describe the washrooms in detail?

Trained mystery shoppers are chosen to match your customer's psychographic and demographic profile. They are local residents, primed with a set of behaviours and facts which customers have said are important and a measurement system which records how well things are done. They are not staff of other companies who may have an ulterior motive and they are not friends of the executive. They are trained to observe and engage your staff in conversation designed to deliver that which you promised in your unique selling proposition. Quality mystery customer programs focus on "why" results occur, not on identifying a single employee. Generally, when our mystery shoppers uncover poor service, the real reason lies somewhere further up the corporate ladder.

OBJECTIVE: To create a mystery customer program.

PROCESS: To create the service steps in your organization, answer the question: How do customers experience your service delivery? In addition to looking at your perceptions, use focus groups and behavioural observations to find out what customers actually do during a visit to your site. Make sure that staff understand what skills and processes are required to deliver the service steps and have the skills to score "100." It isn't fair to send in mystery shoppers unless staff are able to deliver the experience you are evaluating.

Make sure the shopping team understands what they are looking for and has the skill to create a situation where the staff can show off their training and knowledge. One method is to have the mystery customers fill out a form after viewing a video model. The trainer then discusses the responses of trainees and ensures that everyone understands how to evaluate correctly.

Use the information as a positive learning tool, not as a club. This is as much a score of your performance in delivering the training, staffing, and support as it is an evaluation of any individual. Before you take any action, find out if there are any reasons for the score. One client discovered that a low-performing store was in the middle of a flood. Imagine the consequences to morale if there had been punitive action without investigating first.

TACTIC: Think in terms of benchmark data so you can assess changes over time. Doing a shop before and after a training initiative, or a management change, are two examples. And don't forget to shop the competition, especially the ones that have a high proportion of Monarch Customers!

The people dimension is not only the most critical dimension when it comes to the customer's emotional response to your business, it is the dimension that requires the most attention from you. It is the one most influenced by the values you espouse and the corporate behaviours your company displays.

How your staff are affected by their working environment has a great bearing on their ability to make the impersonal, personal; to deliver the appropriate service strategy and deliver it consistently.

In companies that enjoy a high percentage of loyal, trusting Monarch Customers, we usually find a high degree of trust in the employees as well. They trust that the values so clearly stated will be lived out in the daily behaviours of the leaders and other members of the team. They trust that the workings of the organization are designed to allow them to perform their best. They live their working life in an environment which is harmonious. There is no culture clash between what they are being asked to give to customers and what they have to live with themselves.

Internal Affairs

ARE YOU TRYING to create a seamless experience for the customer while forcing your employees to operate in a fragmented, disjointed world? Do you tell customers everything they need to know while keeping secrets from your staff? Do you talk as if the customer comes first, while always acting in the interests of the shareholder? Culture clash happens when the reality of a company's internal affairs are in direct contradiction to the seamless, harmonious, trustworthy whole beloved of Monarchs. A culture clash makes a discordant sound indeed.

WHAT IS CORPORATE CULTURE?

This term, for us who see things feelingly, describes the ephemeral, but very real soul of a company. It is the way individuals working in the entity intuitively know they have to act in order to fit in or be at home. You can "feel" culture on the front lines, in remote operating units, and in the executive office. Think of it as the way your organization would instinctively behave under stress. If threatened, would you hunker down and protect your assets, or strike out offensively? Would the team gather together or split apart? Would communications dry up or improve? If operating numbers dive is the first reaction to cut costs, or try to increase sales? Or, maybe your corporate style is to turn to analysis before deciding what action to take.

The search for gaps and disharmony begins and ends with the internal affairs of a company. In Chapter Seven we started the presentation of common gaps with "no strategy" and discussed how difficult harmony is when an organization is not focused, faithful, flexible, or fast in how it operates. Throughout the remaining chapters, themes of "involving the front-line employees" and "singing from the same song sheet" stressed how creating a trustworthy environment depends on these things being a matter of course.

And so we come to the gap that may underlie all the others. It is the gap that occurs when a company's internal operating style is in direct conflict with the values required to build the trust that attracts Monarch Customers. What do we typically find in a company where the culture clashes with the espoused values? We find that decisions affecting the total organization are mostly made in one or two key areas. The interpretation of the strategy or the plan depends on who you ask and leaders have their own rule book.

In this operating environment, managers and staff live daily with Uh-ohs as the dimensions are out of sync and the needs of the stakeholders come into conflict. This is a corporate culture designed to attract Butterflies.

In contrast, what are the profiles of companies whose customers are loyal Monarchs? What characteristics do these organizations display that allow them to create a culture that meets the challenge of providing a pleasing, harmonious experience in a complex, constantly changing world?

As we conduct our audits and help companies to look at their three dimensions with new eyes we find that the ones with high balances in the customer trust account usually display three traits that add up to the right corporate culture.

A 3-D Decision Process: The three dimensions and the three stakeholders are reflected in how people make decisions. The advertising agency would no sooner create a media campaign without input from operations than they would without consulting the CEO. The product development team works with accounting and both are joined at the hip with human resources before finalizing an action plan.

Complete Communications: Everyone in the organization gets the relevant information they need to carry our their part in planning or delivering 3-D harmony. The communications mantra of "no surprises" means that everyone can trust that they will hear what they need to know in time and that the information will be reliable.

3-D Leadership: The leaders set the tone in seeing the business feelingly and taking accountability for the trust account balance and expect everyone else to do the same. There are no double standards when it comes to taking care of the needs of the customers, the employees, and the shareholders.

A 3-D DECISION PROCESS

Get all the stakeholders in the room, at least in spirit, every time a key decision is made. And, get decisions made as close to the action as possible.

Decisions Made in 3-D

Is your organization suffering from a high proportion of great events that fail to deliver on their promise or end up taking you nowhere? You might want to take a look at how they are developed and delivered. When those in charge operate in isolation, decisions take you and your customers all over the place. There may be a disproportionate emphasis on one dimension, such as, the newspaper ads that consume the budget leaving nothing for staff training. Perhaps there are no ways to measure results. Regardless, the consequences are evident to customer and staff alike. The lack of continuity and integration contribute to diminishing trust as the execution fails to live in harmony with the promise. By contrast, what does a 3-D decision-making process look like?

It doesn't matter whether the decision is being made by an individual owner or a large team. Whether it is a committee of one or a team of many, those in charge of the decision move forward only after thinking through the implications for all three dimensions and all three stakeholders. How is this done? By training people to walk through the implications of their decisions in the shoes of others. This can be as simple as forcing people to answer a series of questions before they take action: Which colleagues will be influenced by the decisions about to be made? How might this affect the other stakeholders—customers and shareholders? Will expectations be set-up in the other dimensions? Can the other dimensions deliver those expectations and how can we be sure the answer will be "yes," before customers arrive at the door?

Or, it can be a formal training or orientation program. One client calls theirs "Walk a Mile in my Shoes" and it is designed to show different departments how they depend on one another for success. This knowledge can lead to dramatic changes in behaviour. At one company, the operations folks began to deliver their payroll documentation records with virtually 100% consistency once they understood the negative effect on the accounting team, the employee involved, and profit, when deadlines were missed or information was incomplete.

Take a look at a decision that worked. In other words, one that delivered the expected results and left all three stakeholders feeling good about what happened. We guarantee you will find your own model for decisions in 3-D.

Make Decisions Close To the Action

On the surface, a top-down management style may sound exactly right to create the consistency needed for a great consumer operation across divisions, departments, and even time zones, but in practice, it doesn't work very well. Decisions taken in the rarefied air of an office or corporate headquarters are often out of touch with the viewpoint of those dealing directly with customers.

Decisions need to take place where the action is, as close to the point of customer contact as possible. If decisions aren't being made at that point, ask yourself why.

- Is it because those people would make bad decisions?

   If the answer is "yes," then provide them with the education and insight to make good decisions. There are some ideas about how to do that in Chapter Thirteen.

- Is it because you reward them for not making the decision on their own?

   Each time someone "checks" their decision with you before actually taking action, guess who now owns the decision? You do. It is human nature to act defensively and who can blame anyone for passing the buck when it is willingly accepted? Check your own behaviour to see if there are decisions that end up on your lap that belong to someone else. Push every decision you can closer to the action.

- Is it because it's easier and faster to just do it yourself?

It may be today, but unless you're prepared to do everything yourself from now to eternity, you had better take the time to delegate some of those decisions. Explain, train, and then measure the results. To paraphrase the old proverb, it's better to teach them to fish than remain on the hook for providing the meal.

TIP

OBJECTIVE: To get decisions made when and where they can do the most good.

PROCESS: For one week track every single decision you make or are asked to approve.

For every decision ask: Why was I the one to do this?

If the answer is because you didn't trust the quality of the decision or had information the decision maker needed, take action to fix it through education and training.

If the answer is because somehow, you reward the team for bringing you decisions they could make, then stop!

TACTIC: Ask those bringing you the decisions to document each request for approval and code them as follows:

1) I'm bringing it to you because I don't have enough information.

2) I'm bringing it to you because I thought you wanted to see it before it is implemented.

3) You told me to bring it to you.

4) I don't know why I'm bringing it.

Sort all the items and create a plan to reduce the number of requests for approval brought to you.

COMPLETE COMMUNICATIONS

In response to our questions about decisions, future plans, results of their actions, and rating of their performance, employees tell us "How do I know?" "I don't know, they don't tell me." "They treat me like a mushroom...you know, keep me in the dark and feed me s--t!"

If your culture is rife with gossip and much time is wasted trying to find out what is going on and then confirming that which was learned is actually going on, welcome to your own personal mushroom farm. This is *not* an environment designed to build trust with the customer or anyone else, for that matter.

If you want to bring light and air to your employees, here are four simple rules.

1. Send messages that match.
2. Confirm the message is received.
3. Design them for the receiver.
4. Send them at the appropriate time.

Send Messages that Match

Just like the Butterfly Customer, employees have finely attuned antennae that are on alert for inconsistency in any form. Picture this. An executive who has just told us he wants to institute some draconian policies because he thinks his customers are trying to rip him off, hands over a company mission statement that says "the care and nurture of the customer is the company's reason for being." The internal newsletter is filled with exhortations from the president to "take care of the customer" while the branch manager's e-mail features a directive to cut staff hours. And so on.

Periodically take a moment and read a few memos sent to the front lines, notices posted in the back room, or on computer bulletin boards of your organization. Are they in line with your values, strategy, and current activities in the three dimensions? Do the messages you're sending to staff match what you say to customers or to other stakeholders? If not, fix it.

Confirm the Message Is Received

"Many a slip, twixt the cup and the lip" is an accurate description of the gap that exists between what is said and what is understood. Are the messages in your organization distorted as they travel from you to the field and vice versa?

Have you ever played the telephone game where a message is privately passed from person to person until the originator finally hears the by-now garbled version? Usually all the players are astounded to hear how just a few words can be so quickly transmuted into a completely different meaning.

And yet traditionally in a service business, that is how information is given and received as successive layers interpret and homogenize the communication into garbled pablum. How do you avoid the trap? There is only one infallible test to ensure the receiver has the same message as the sender. Demonstration.

When it comes to messages you are sending, the indicator of an appropriately communicated, well understood, and living 3-D corporate culture is that all of the organization can give examples and demonstrate behaviours that indicate an understanding of the three dimensions in harmony and how the needs of the three stakeholders are being met. On one of your forays into the world of your employees and customers, gather your own evidence through questions and observations that the understanding of the message by those who receive it, is exactly the same as for those who sent it.

And how about the messages you are receiving? Apply the method in reverse. Give employees and customers your understanding of what they are telling you through the various channels and make sure their message hasn't been interpreted out of existence.

Design Them for the Receiver

How much is too much communication? You will never cross that line if what you do is relevant and timely. Interesting is also good. These are messages that have been designed with the receiver in mind.

It's too bad more corporations aren't run by graduates of communications programs. If they were, we might see corporate communications filled with the variety and creativity which ensure people pay attention and learn. Look at the e-mail message system or back room in most service organizations and weep. Text is everywhere and, in the computer format, unrelieved by even basic design principles. Surf the Internet, take a look at television, read *Wired* and see how many different ways there are to say the same thing. If you find yourself constantly repeating the same message, maybe you need to look at a new way to deliver it.

But more important than interesting is relevant. One of our favourite exercises was described in Chapter Six. We put ourselves on the internal mailing list and bury ourselves in the boxes of ensuing communication. Here is one way we help organizations fight their way through the paper jungle, and prune the communications to the ones that really are relevant and timely.

We force the executive or operating committee to sit down with a sample of all the recent of internal communications and ask them to:

a) explain how the memo benefits any or all of the stakeholders;

b) describe the action the receiver should take as a result of the communication; and

c) well actually, we rarely get to (c) because the point is made. Relevancy, like beauty has to be in the eye of the beholder.

Send Them at the Appropriate Time

Relevant and interesting communications are important, but timing messages, as in life, is everything. Why is it that so many companies which wouldn't let a week go by without telling customers what is going on in their business, through flyers, ads, or in-store signage, let staff go for months without any real information? How come the bank knows that gross margin is slipping but the staff (who could do something about it) doesn't?

Once upon a time, "Saturday morning meetings" were a fixture of the retail scene. These brief powwows brought together the entire staff with their manager to catch up on company news. They shared information that morning which could be used immediately. As part of the overall imperative to cut costs, these occasions to share information, reward achievements, and generally get ready for some of the busiest hours of the week have all but disappeared. That in and of itself is not a bad thing, provided it is replaced with some other method of communicating.

While it may be expensive to get everyone together weekly, it is more expensive not to have a format for sharing timely information, rewarding achievements, and focusing the team on new objectives for performance, productivity, and service. Uninformed employees are incapable employees and create an environment where harmony cannot flourish and the sound of the clash is deafening.

Increased use of part-time workers and longer operating hours make meetings and communication expensive but it's one investment you can't afford to avoid. You pay for maintenance of the other assets of the business so why not maintain the most valuable one of all…your people?

One successful independent store owner we know has a "no more than 30 days" meetings rule. At least once in that time period he pays overtime to have staff stay an extra half-hour after closing. Why do his staff prompt him to hold these meetings? So they can stay an extra half-hour after the end of a busy day? Hardly! It sure isn't because they want to earn the extra five dollars. It is because the owner makes the meetings fun, rewarding, and interesting. They learn the big picture strategy and are drawn into a sense of ownership by being invited to offer suggestions and identify areas of opportunity. They are engaged in the planning process for media campaigns and promotions. There is a great deal of research that confirms the positive effects on customers of having informed, involved, and in control staff.

Timely, relevant, and interesting, if these adjectives describe your communications you will find a positive effect on the decision-making ability of the company. And then, when others are making most of the decisions and everyone has sufficient information, what's your role? What do you have to do to create a culture that delivers in 3-D?

3-D LEADERSHIP

In these times of organizational "flattening" when layers of managers have been removed, more responsibility is placed on the leader. In a 3-D culture this means leaders who unerringly see the customer's experience feelingly. They set a high standard by matching what they do with what they say and when things go wrong worry most about their own behaviour and the influence they generate. There have been many examples in the last five chapters about how to see the business feelingly. In this section we will focus on two other attributes of a leader in a harmonious culture.

Walk the Talk

When we do a 3-D Audit, our first activity is to interview the executive of the corporation. They tell us what values, beliefs, guiding principles, and mission the company embraces. They drag out pristine (a sure hint that no one has touched it since it was printed) mission statements and swear that this is the guiding light, the direction, and the basis of the culture of the corporation. We then ask for examples of their own corporate behaviour that they believe embody the culture they espouse.

Now, get out your mission statement (or whatever it is called) and answer the following question: What are the things you have done in the last twenty-four hours that demonstrate to those observing you (and your employees) that you are one of those leaders who "walks their talk"?

In the interview, we would record your responses and then go and ask people in every position in your company the same question: What has your leader done lately that demonstrates the culture of this company? It is often at this point, that the client gets a little uncomfortable and asks, "What has all this to do with improving customer service anyway?"

It has to do with building trust. Do you want to see customer service sabotage on a large scale? Simply visit any service floor where staff are being turned inside out trying to accomplish some impossible objective while being told how important the customers are. One retailer agonized for years about getting staff to wear badges. It wasn't until they realized that everyone who asked a staff member to wear a badge was without one, that they realized what the real problem was. Do as I do, is always more powerful than do as I say.

OBJECTIVE: To see how you walk the talk through others' eyes.

PROCESS: Go ahead and do this research on your own.

Begin by getting out the documents that describe the corporate culture.

Next, list things you personally have done which exemplify those beliefs.

Now, go and ask some employees to tell you some of your actions that they have experienced first-hand which support the company culture.

TACTIC: Reverse the old, "What have you done for me lately" theme. Pick a half day next week and go through the office and into the field asking "What have I done for you lately?" And, don't stop inside. Go and ask some customers (don't forget vendors and suppliers) what the company has done for them lately.

If you're not prepared to walk it then don't talk it. When is the last time you did the most important job in the company? Would a customer served by you find you adding value to their experience? How did employees and customers benefit from what you did today?

Fix Your Own Mistakes

The results of a mystery customer program (the service measurement technique discussed in Chapter Eleven), can reveal a great deal about the accountability style of an organization. It is always surprising to hear the owner's response to any examples of less than perfect service. "The reason the wait at the reservation counter was so long is that we were short of staff that day" or "We had a great day and we were busier than we expected" or "Yes but, there was a huge shipment of merchandise arriving at the time you sent the mystery customer in" or "That was the day our equipment was down." One of our favourites is, "Who served you?" as if the customer should know not to go near certain employees.

Who is responsible for these things anyway? Instead of spending all that energy thinking about what someone else may have done or not done, take a look at your own job description. Don't you have a responsibility to provide adequate staffing, training, or inventory? And, for making sure those things are perfect? There may be lots to fix in your own job description before tackling how well the next person is delivering theirs.

A 3-D COMPANY

The culture of a 3-D company thrives when decisions take into account the needs of all three dimensions and all three stakeholders; when communications are relevant, timely, and understood by the receiver; and when leaders walk their talk. But an organization is only a collection of individuals. And, in the service and retail sector a high proportion of these employees are constantly on the move from one employer to the next. How do you mold the individual employees who will form the team that will thrive in the culture you have created, a team of individuals poised to be successful in a 3-D company, in a 3-D world, a team of service-empowered people?

CHAPTER THIRTEEN

The Service-Empowered Team

If you want one year of prosperity, grow grain

If you want ten years of prosperity, grow trees

If you want one hundred years of prosperity, grow people.

Chinese Proverb[1]

REGARDLESS OF THE exact design of your unique selling proposition or service strategy, if you want prosperity, you need to learn to grow people. And not just any old people will do when it comes to creating an environment which attracts Monarch Customers. You need people who can make decisions close to the action, make the impersonal, personal for the customer when it comes to service, and contribute good ideas to the corporate plan. And, you need them to do this regardless of their distance from the head office or length of service with the company.

---

[1] As quoted in James M. Kouzes, and Barry Z. Posner, *The Leadership Challenge: How to Get Extraordinary Things Done in Organizations* (San Francisco: Jossey-Bass, 1987).

To deliver 3-D harmony, you have to be prepared to let employees "own" their actions and the consequences. You have to let go of delivering the three dimensions personally and empower your people to not only protect the trust already in your account but to go out and inspire customers to make additional deposits.

WHAT ARE EMPOWERED PEOPLE?

Employee empowerment may be one of the most misunderstood, and therefore abused, concepts in customer service today. Somehow management developed the notion that one could simply hand over responsibility for customer satisfaction to front-line individuals and everything would come out fine. After all, wasn't the ticket agent who escorted the passenger halfway across the terminal an "empowered" employee? Wasn't she doing whatever she could to turn the customer into a raving fan?

What happened in the industry was that after letting go, executives and owners watched in horror as employees made inappropriate decisions that cost shareholders, customers, and other employees. When management tried to hold individuals accountable, their defence was solid and immutable, "I can't get inside your head to figure out what you would have done" and "I did the best I could." It's no wonder we are beginning to see the leaders grabbing back the reins, to protect the business.

But hanging onto the reins is no answer, either. If ever there was a retailer who learned their lesson the hard way in this regard it was Joey Basmaji of Boutique Jacob, a spirited, family-owned women's fashion chain based in Montreal.

For many years the business had been very successful in capturing the loyalty of young Quebec women with its affordable, European-chic clothing and image-oriented media campaign. But when the business moved beyond the Quebec borders, cracks appeared. The transition, which at first appeared smooth, soon revealed a business far from ready to translate its successful unique selling proposition in Quebec, into a system that would be as efficient in locations thousands of miles, a couple of time zones, and almost a different world away.

As is often the case, what turned out to be a key problem was part of the company's initial success: Joey's informal approach to structuring and managing its people. Like many entrepreneurs, Basmaji always stuck close to the company's daily operations. He was a key player in every single game going on in the organization. His was a management-by-walking-around style, using his insatiable curiosity to uncover and fix problems and grabbing opportunities as they arose. The plan, according to him, was that there was no plan. "You wander around knowing that you'll pick something up along the way. Our philosophy was that we knew where we were going, but not directly how we would get there or how long it would take."

Joey's desire to grow the business beyond his personal span of control was in conflict with the need to hang on to the details to protect what was already built. A 3-D Audit uncovered evidence in the structural foundation and day-to-day operations that indicated why he couldn't let go, even though he wanted to. What was it that was getting in the way?

No job descriptions. Imagine a service business operating in two languages, over three thousand miles, with no job descriptions and no individual accountability except for Joey and a couple of other executives. The lack of formal accountability contributed to an environment where regional managers were glorified supervisors, supervisors behaved like store managers, and managers ran around doing tasks on the selling floor.

The field lacked Joey's instincts. The young team wanted to please him and did everything they were told to the best of their ability. They interpreted his ideas and objectives through their

own unskilled eyes. What they lacked was Joey's knack of quickly identifying and solving gaps and disharmony. He saw the business feelingly but hadn't figured out how to transfer that ability to
his neophyte team.

Limited training. The stores ran with no formal training. Sure,
managers knew how to open and close the doors, but they had no
clue about how to protect the business, much less grow it. Nor
were they rewarded for growing the business.

Rewards but no consequences. As often happens with a youth-
oriented organization, Basmaji had become the "parent" to many
of the staff. We found evidence of a lot of "Let's please Daddy"
behaviour going on. And being the kind, benevolent father that he
was, Basmaji had a difficult time making hard decisions when it
came to his "children." Hence, employees who were not contributing were being rewarded the same as ones who were.

What Joey needed was to create an organization filled with
Joey-clones. People who, regardless of the distance from the head
office, would see the business as feelingly and totally as he did;
have the curiosity to find out why and then fix-it mentality to take
responsibility for actions. He needed a team of people who would
share his knowledge and skills so he could trust their advice and
decisions, and like him, share in the rewards of getting it right, or
the consequences of getting it wrong. In order to let go of the now-
impossible task of *personally* delivering the three dimensions, he
needed a team of service-empowered people.

WHAT ARE SERVICE-EMPOWERED PEOPLE?

Service-empowered people are those who have understanding (of
the big picture), insight (into the roles of the three stakeholders),
knowledge (about the company, its products, and the job they are
required to perform), and skill (at a level sufficient to ensure they
can perform successfully in a variety of situations). They need all

of these things to see the business feelingly from the perspectives of all three stakeholders and understand the implications of their decisions on all three dimensions.

Imagine the power of hundreds of clones of you. Imagine every employee seeing your business feelingly and making decisions the way you would. While there is no single set of human resource practices that companies with a high proportion of Monarch Customers have in common, there are some approaches which most share. Here is what they do:

Job descriptions: A recognition of each position's relationship to the rest of the organization (three dimensions) and a desire to satisfy all three stakeholders are found in every job description of every employee, from the newly hired part-timer to chairman of the board.

Selection: These companies have, through a controlled selection process, acquired a significant percentage of employees who share the traits that distinguish those who thrive in an operating environment designed to engender trust.

Education: Beyond training and development, these employees are invited to understand the business of the business. They know the real profit numbers and what to do to change them. They are educated in the moods of the customer and can impress you with their knowledge of the competition.

Rewards and Punishment: Employees at all levels can cite examples of behaviours that would have a positive or negative effect on any or all of the three stakeholders and the resultant reward or consequence. It is clear to all concerned when each is deserved.

OBJECTIVE: A sound human resource system.

PROCESS: Select people who are likely to be successful doing this job in your environment.

Train them in the skills and knowledge they will need to do the work well.

Ensure they know what they are accountable for and the rewards and consequences that can be expected.

In each of the four sections below, we will provide a quick snapshot of the human resource basics. If you find your current system lacking in any of these regards, get help.

TACTIC: If you do not have a human resource department (those devoted to helping individuals do their best in your organization) then you might want to contact your local personnel or training and development association, or trade association, and ask for the names of some companies that can help you design such a system. Additionally, there are many consultants with experience in companies similar to yours who, through downsizing, are now on their own, and willing to do this on a contractual basis.

EVERYONE HAS A 3-D JOB DESCRIPTION

Whether formal or informal, job or position descriptions should be based on accountability and focused on outcomes, rather than tasks. It doesn't seem to matter so much if the description is written formally in management by objective style or done more casually; the key is to focus on "what is to be achieved" rather than "how to achieve it." Believe it or not, a job description can even be communicated verbally but those in writing are a better reference point and can be referred to in discussions about performance.

Accountability-based job descriptions help to ensure everyone knows why they have been hired and therefore how to measure their own success on the job. To assess if you have accountability-based job descriptions, think of the job of someone who reports to you. Now, write down one outcome you expect as a result of this person's performance. Stop! If you said "making sales" or "serving customers" you had better go back a chapter or two. Making sales isn't an outcome but a measure, and serving customers is a tactic intended to deliver the outcome. If you find yourself with a measure ask, "What will the person be doing that will deliver the result?" Your tactics are things like serving, merchandising, planning, and selling. To move from tactics to accountability, ask "Why do we serve customers?" To ensure they buy today and want to return tomorrow. That is what the employee is accountable for.

OK, now ask: "Does the employee know this outcome is expected of them and why it is important to the customers? Can they identify the indicators that tell them when it is well done?" If not, you may be focusing employees more on the "how" rather than the "why." Or, worse, giving them no focus at all.

Service-Empowered Job Descriptions

Everyone has an accountability to protect the trust account with the customer, and that means everyone needs to watch for disharmony and shadows. And, everyone has an obligation to all three stakeholders—making this a good place for customers to do business, a good place for all employees to do productive, satisfying work, and an attractive place for shareholders or owners to invest their capital.

In an organization that really understands the concept we would find the same accountabilities in all the job descriptions. For instance, at Jacob, everyone has a responsibility for protecting assets. How can the chief operating officer have the same responsibility as the person just hired? Easy, they each carry the accountability of looking after the needs of all three stakeholders. It is just the scope of command that changes.

While the executive looks far into the future and the front line deals with the reality of the present, all are focused on delivering an integrated experience to the customer and meeting the needs of all three stakeholders. Everyone understands their interdependence on one another, where to go with or for information, and the importance of timing. The customer help-desk clerk who hears two callers in a week talk about how much "better" the telephone system is at the competitors, knows the value of that information and who to report it to. And there is an established process for doing so. From the other perspective, a consumer trend heard by an executive at an industry workshop can often be confirmed in minutes by consulting the front line.

Focus everyone in the business to think about their accountability to each customer and how every action and decision has an effect on all the three dimensions. It's good for the customer, good for the employee, and it's likely to be good for the shareholder as well.

PEOPLE ARE SELECTED BECAUSE THEY WILL THRIVE

This increasingly sophisticated aspect of human resource management is still all about matching the right person to the right job. Since the best predictor of future behaviour is still past performance, make sure your selection process gets at evidence of past performance. Make sure those who hire others in your company can tell you exactly what they look for in a candidate and how they know they have found it. Make sure they are looking for evidence that the candidate delivered the output rather than concentrating on "how" they did it. If you are selecting based on gut feeling or some other outmoded system, you aren't putting the best talent at your disposal.

Seek out others in the industry who have the reputation for hiring right and ask them to share their process and selection criteria with you. For example, if you are in a seasonal business where you have to hire scads of people in a short period of time, then Disney, which hires thousands of seasonal people every year, would be one service organization to study.

Service-Empowered Selection Criteria

What are the innate characteristics of employees who thrive in the organization which delivers consistent 3-D harmony? There are two traits found in a high percentage of employees of organizations that build trust. While they may be demonstrated in different ways in the fast pace of the front line than they are in the executive suite, these traits are, in fact, shared by all. The first is curiosity.

Curiosity Keeps This Cat Alive

Why is curiosity such a valued trait? Because without it, the ever-changing customer will be viewed through yesterday's glasses. The little glitches that appear in the systems and procedures will be ignored until they turn into a full-blown problem. The customer who says, "I used to come here all the time" won't be asked what made them stop and what brought them back. Employees without curiosity can unpack a carton of merchandise without really seeing any of the contents. And without curiosity, employees accept instructions at face value instead of asking why.

Although often more difficult to manage, curious employees are worth their weight in gold. Send them out to learn about your competition and they will come back with information you never dreamed possible to acquire. Turn them loose on customer research and they will come back with information as valuable as that from an expensive study.

OBJECTIVE: To uncover the curiosity trait.

PROCESS: Since past behaviour is the best predictor of future actions, you want to gain evidence of a candidate's use of curiosity. Do this by developing a set of questions that require the respondent to tell you of a time when they were curious about something, what steps they took to satisfy their curiosity, and the results of their actions. You want to know if the person has both the desire to know and the skill to find out effectively.

TACTIC: Use questions that begin with "Tell me about a time when..." Ask why certain things are done in their existing job. Or, create a situation that requires curiosity and ask: "How would you handle this situation?" There are also inexpensive surveys and tests which can be administered to determine the level of curiosity of an individual.

When You Win, I Win

Unlike the first trait which can be described in a single adjective that means the same thing to everyone, the second trait is more difficult to describe, but is just as powerful in action. It is the desire to be of service to others. By service we don't mean to "go below stairs" and wait to be called upon like the servants in times of old.

It is rather a genuine joy in participating in solving a problem, meeting a need, offering a kindness to a stranger, and finding the act its own reward.

In organizations with a team dedicated to serving, we find an accounting clerk excited about developing a new payroll system that saves supervisory time, buyers who thrive on the moments they interact with customers, an executive who sneaks in time to work on an industry task force, and front-line staff who stop on their way to lunch to help a colleague. We find individuals who think that helping someone else is a neat thing to do and can't help but find ways to do it.

Like curiosity, this trait can be uncovered with good interviewing techniques and aptitude tests. Look for situations where a person has the opportunity to be of service. The things you want to hear are that they take a genuine pleasure in being of service; they indicate self-fulfillment from problem solving; they have great listening skills; and are willing to give credit to others. Things you don't want to hear are things that indicate that they have a low opinion of customers. It's amazing how many service providers really dislike serving customers.

While knowledge and skill are the basics of a selection program, service-empowered people also bring some innate traits that can help your company and your customers.

EDUCATION: BEYOND TRAINING AND DEVELOPMENT

In these times of rapid change, your success depends on employees who can quickly analyse and assess, and make appropriate decisions. Traditional training, which focused on teaching someone how to accomplish a specific task, isn't enough. Empowered employees, in addition to task training, also need to be educated in the business of business. They need to be able to rationally process information and arrive at brand-new ways of meeting the needs of the ever-changing customer. An education teaches people how to think.

Training and Development Basics

"All too often, decisions are made to build new stores, to buy new technology, or to start a new promotion without any consideration as to what that same money would do if spent on training and development of employees in the company." [2]

It is much easier to spend money on bricks and mortar than on a human asset because the delivery is immediate; you see it in weeks instead of years. The result is visible; you can see and feel where the money went. The outcome is predictable; you know what you will get for your money. You can even predict the maintenance cycle.

But it isn't when it comes to people. They don't all respond the same way to the same initiatives. They are free agents, and an attempt at a human "renovation," or training investment, may actually end up benefiting the competition if your staff turnover is high. Perhaps that is why one retailer we interviewed said he, "wouldn't put the staff in training until they had proved their staying power by lasting three months!" Imagine! For three months customers are in the hands of an untrained person.

And, as if that weren't bad enough, consider peak traffic periods; those lunchtime, after-work, or weekend periods when the maximum number of consumers experience your business. It's when the part-timer is typically scheduled and given control of your business so that the full-timer (the one with the seniority

---

[2] Michael J. O'Connor, "International Trends in Retailing newsletter," Arthur Anderson & Co.

who possesses all the knowledge about your product and presentation) can go home. It's like assigning a pilot-in-training to the flight that is expecting a stormy turbulent ride. Why is this so prevalent in the service sector when it is so obviously wrong?

Maybe it's because a great deal of money has been spent on training in the past only to deliver insignificant results. All too often, the training is poorly designed or more likely, the wrong training is delivered. Do you remember the client in Chapter One whose employees were trained to give the customer "warm fuzzies"? The employees were great at smiling but they couldn't explain products or policies to customers.

Another reason we find a deficiency in training is that it is treated like an inoculation—once is enough. "Oh, our employees already had that training," is a common response when we suggest that there is a lack of communication skills or knowledge of a goal-setting process. Yes, but they aren't using it. Did you know that up to 80% of all training dollars are wasted if the learning is never followed up or coached? This fact may be the reason why business is so reluctant to invest in any more training...the last round didn't stick.

Here are the basics you should look for when you evaluate your training system.

1. Employees are trained before being let loose on customers.

2. The training is designed to match the needs of the learners. Fundamentals are stressed, and there are refreshers and reminders to keep the team in top performance. Knowledge-based training includes examples and practical applications. Skill training allows an opportunity to rehearse.

3. The responsibility for protecting the training investment is placed in the front line. The supervisor or coach, not the training department, needs to be accountable for the employees' use of their new skills or knowledge.

Service-Empowered Training

Beyond those basics, what kinds of education and development do we find in an organization of service-empowered people? There are three:

1. Orientation to the Vision and Culture

2. Education About Business

3. Understanding About Customers

Orientation to the Vision and Culture

Everyone needs to understand the vision, the strategy, and their role in the plan, and they need to know it within the first few hours of starting work. Better yet, it should be the *first* thing they learn when they start work. It's amazing that we even have to discuss orientation, but it is one of the issues raised most often in the 3-D Audit. In what, on the outside, appear to be very large and very sophisticated organizations, we find employees (many well past the probationary period) who can't articulate the company goals, philosophy, or beliefs. They had little or no orientation and what was called orientation was often little more than task training. Orientation is your chance to demonstrate that your culture is committed to people and that they are your most important resource.

The orientation need not be formal or facilitator-led to be effective. One client had a group of employees in one of their outpost operations, create their own "Guide to the questions employees want to know." This manual is well-thumbed in every part of the organization.

Education About Business

Educate every employee in the aspects of margins, profit, and return on investment. Is it worth sharing such sensitive information? Just ask New Brunswick Tourism whose summer employees quickly figured out how their behaviour could help meet the provincial objective of "getting customers to stay a little longer and spend a little more" when they were asked to create a business plan for a fictional Tourist Information Centre. Employees can plan their own actions better when they understand the implications for the business.

We give our retail clients a simple little program for use with their new front-line employees. It's called "Welcome to Retail" and in order to deliver the program to the staff, the client has to share gross margin, expenses, and profit numbers. This act, often uncomfortable at the start, is later frequently credited as being a primary contributor to the increased effectiveness and contribution to profit of the front line.

Understanding About Customers

Employees who think like customers provide valuable information and make better decisions. Every one of your employees is a customer to somebody and you need to find a way to help them see your business through those same critical eyes. One way to increase that ability is to send them out to experience a "foreign" environment in the shoes of the customer. And when you are a gas retailer you can't go to an environment much more foreign than a lingerie boutique! What could those who sell gasoline and convenience products learn from a visit to a specialty women's store?

They learned about customer discomfort and as a result were able to look at their own sites and find ways to make new or infrequent users feel more at home. They saw that new technology designed to speed the transaction, led to customers arriving at their sites with higher expectations. And, they saw first-hand how customers wander all over the retail map in unexpected ways.

Next, a visit to their own competition helped uncover opportunity areas where they could improve their service at little or no additional cost and move ahead of the competition as they looked at merchandising, product mix, and service. The learning from getting out into the field had immediate and practical impact as they returned with "fresh eyes." The resulting increase in mystery shop scores confirmed that the learning had translated into quicker service and offers of extra service.

Beyond the basics of good training and development, a company that wants service-empowered people makes education and learning a way of life, from the first orientation session, through to sharing facts about the business, to ongoing activities to learn about customers. This is a team that is ready to be held accountable, take the consequences for creating Uh-ohs and shadows, and ready to share in the rewards of building trust and delivering harmony to all three stakeholders.

REWARDS AND CONSEQUENCES

Employees thrive on recognition and reward. Not just pay, but recognition. Of course you have to be competitive in your compensation package, but the big difference between companies with great internal morale and those with poor morale often seems to be related to the reward system. In companies with high morale, there is great pleasure in achievements, lots of public recognition, and there are also swift and predictable consequences for non-performance.

There are many companies that specialize in designing reward and consequence systems. The important thing is that employee and management alike understand why a reward is earned or a consequence deserved.

Service-Empowered Rewards and Consequences

An advanced system puts the information about performance into the hands of the empowered team. They are the first to learn if they are on their way to a reward, or about to suffer a consequence. And, they know what each will be.

When a bonus cheque is received, or a reprimand given, the empowered employee is not surprised, knows what was done to get this feedback, and is already planning future action.

Rewards and consequences should be tied to outcomes which please all three stakeholders, not just the shareholder. As discussed in Chapter Seven, to be faithful to your strategy requires attention to the needs of all. Employees who are rewarded only for "making sales" understand exactly what is important and which stakeholder they are pleasing: the shareholder. Want an alternative measure to focus the team? What about an instant gratification mystery shop program?

Instead of using ubiquitous mystery customers as cops, let them offer instant rewards for service that exceeds expectations. At Blue Mountain Resorts in Ontario, an ounce of silver (retail value $10) might have been pure gold considering the reaction our mystery customers received from even the most "seasoned" ski resort staff. The grapevine buzzed as staff earned the silver and heard directly from the mystery customers what behaviour had earned the reward. From handing out cash to retail sales people for demonstrating an advertised product, to giving a franchisee recognition for a great display, having a program to reward front-line activities pays off.

The service-empowered team understands how the rewards and consequences are tied into the overall strategy and what can be done to affect results. The system is not only fair, it is perceived to be fair.

IT IS TIME TO LET GO

All of the service-empowering practices in the world don't count for much if the organization is not prepared to turn over decisions and accountability. You can't have the benefits of all those clones unless you hand over the reins to people you may never meet. But what will it take to give you the confidence that it is safe to do so? We discussed Joey Basmaji of Jacob earlier in this chapter. What finally convinced him to let go?

The Protective Parent Finally Lets Go

The process, which began for Jacob in 1990, is ongoing. The first year was spent putting a game plan in place; the second year was a transitional one, moving from the old culture to the new. By the third year a major difference was apparent that set Jacob apart from other Canadian fashion retailers.

Where else would you find a group of a hundred young (average age about 23) retail managers who could accurately predict their business? As a reward for a profitable year all managers and trainees were invited to Montreal to spend a few days with Joey and the head office team. As an exercise, they had been asked to take all the knowledge and skills they had acquired over the previous two years, evaluate their business, and come prepared to work on creating a sales and store contribution forecast for the coming season. And come prepared they did, with customer information, competitive information, ideas from their colleagues back at the store, and ideas of their own.

In their round-table discussions, store by store, region by region, they put together their plans and translated those plans into sales figures and delivered their predictions to Joey in creative presentations. Joey accepted their forecast and agreed that these numbers would become the financial measure of their success. The real objective was to measure the success of the previous two years' work. How well did these managers really know their business?

The outcome? Less than a quarter of one percent variance was recorded between the collective predictions of 100 young managers and the final numbers. Now that's a measure of success.

"Front line is bottom line," says Basmaji. "We are very comfortable where we are positioned today. We are on time with everything we set out to do."

Formal structures and skilled managers now allow Basmaji to deal with the big picture of the company with the security that the business is being seen through his eyes. He can relax and allow others in the organization to deal with the details of making the big picture work. "It permits me to slow up and see the game in a different way...If we hadn't embarked on this journey, hadn't put the processes in place, we wouldn't have the level of success we have today...Product is something, but it's only a part of the success. Our most important aspect is our people and they were worth the investment."

Perhaps, more importantly, the process allowed the company to formalize its values. "We want our employees to trust themselves first. We have developed a system that builds their self-esteem, teaches them to stand up and speak out, gives them a learning experience they can take with them if they move on...If staff are confident in themselves, they will give that to other people, customers, family, and friends. If front-line staff have the company's trust then they in turn have the confidence to gain the customer's trust."

Do you have an organization which creates service-empowered people? Do you reward staff for identifying shadows in the service delivery? Do you encourage them to eliminate the Uh-Ohs before they happen? Do you ask them for their solutions and invite them to conduct market research with their customers? Do you send them to evaluate the competition and do you listen, listen, listen to what they have to say?

When the customers arrive at your business filled with anticipation that their expectations will be met, who will they find in charge of your business? Will they find employees who have been service empowered and operating in an aligned organization with a clear strategy? Will these employees be in touch with customer expectations, and able to execute a flawless, harmonious experience in all three dimensions?

The answer is in your hands.

CHAPTER FOURTEEN

Exercises in 3-D

So, NOW THAT it's in your hands, we'll bet you're looking for the list of ten steps or five rules to follow in order to do all this 3-D stuff. You know, the one that would so often appear at this point in a business or customer-service book. Just where is that list in this book? In the same place we relegated the superhuman service feats, the Butterfly nets, the expensive programs, and the other easy answers which have failed to satisfy the Butterfly Customer in the last decades. The dustbin! We offer no apology for leaving you without a linear format to follow. The world in which your customers live and experience you is inside/outside, up/down, right/left, and altogether multidimensional. Throw away the notion of simple-minded rule books and follow where your subconscious takes you. Enter into the exciting, mesmerizing, and complete world of the three dimensions.

If you do nothing else as a result of reading this book, just for one day, lose the filters of the numbers, the reports, the consultants, the researchers, and *feel* your business. Experience the emotional roller coaster ride sitting in the same seat as your customer. Live the daily grind in the shoes of the staff who serve the customer and imagine the benefits to the shareholders of a company built on harmony and trust. How do you learn to let yourself see the business feelingly, to think in terms of the business kaleidoscope, to intuitively understand how your business is making your stakeholders feel?

Dig down and get in touch with your own feelings as you go about the business of being someone else's customer. Feel the experience, raise the feeling up to your conscious, and look at it from every possible viewpoint. To do this will cost you nothing but a little time and a new perspective. In other words, "See the business feelingly."

Throughout the book we have offered a series of tips designed to help you feel your business through the eyes of all three stakeholders. Just follow those tips and most importantly, follow your instincts because, once experienced, clients tell us it is hard to imagine doing business without the image of a 3-D world. The depth of perception, understanding, and insight is too valuable to ever set aside.

But what about long term? What is required to keep that sensitivity at its peak? How easy is it to slide back into a unidimensional world where strategy is developed without context, decisions are taken in isolation, and attaining customer trust becomes just one more item on the "to do" list?

It's altogether too easy, in the urgency of the decision-making moment, to slip back to the old perspective. Oh sure, you may experience the beginnings of a shadow when you realize the new ad campaign has been created without any consultation with the front-line staff or has made no allowance for staff training. You may even predict an Uh-oh as customers are incited to join a data base you intend to resell, in order to measure their "loyalty," or employees are only trained after they have survived three months probation. But the roar of the immediate need makes it easy to ignore those inner thoughts. How do you resist the temptation to slip back into old patterns?

You have to wonder as you wander, setting aside the linear in favour of the circuitous. Avoid the singular and focus on the whole. Give emotions equal time with analysis. Learn to be as instinctive as Anita Roddick, Sam Walton, Judy George, Dan Miles, Joey Basmaji, or Warren Rubin are as they explore their customer's emotional landscape.

Just as the award-winning athlete routinely practices basic disciplines, you must practice seeing your business feelingly and the following exercises are ones which our clients report help keep their "feeling muscles" in shape.

Here is the design. First, there is a *set-up* or situation in which you need to imagine yourself, or better yet, actually experience. Next is a series of *top of mind questions* to get you thinking about your reactions. Following that are *subconscious probes* into how you feel and why. And finally, there are some *learning applications* to help you translate the exercise into something you can do in your business.

The exercises are designed around some of the key themes of the book. They are:

1. *Seeing Things Feelingly: The Subconscious Recorder.*

   What do you really notice and record when you are a customer?

2. *Trust: Monarch or Butterfly?*

   Explore which one you really are and why.

3. *Strategy: The Crystal Ball.*

   How you are feeling today may indicate the path forward for tomorrow.

4. *The Service Kaleidoscope: Snapshots in 3-D.*

   Always keep your eyes open for new ideas.

5. *A 3-D Company: Empowered or Entrapped?*

   A simple way to feel what it's like to be your newest employee, and the customer served by them.

EXERCISE #1 SEEING THINGS FEELINGLY: THE SUBCONSCIOUS RECORDER

Just how much do you really see when you are a customer? Listen to your personal subconscious recorder.

The Set-up

Pretend you are asked to describe a McDonald's restaurant to the first visitor from Mars. This curious soul wants to know everything you do about the restaurant. Take a few moments and describe all the facets of the experience. It may amaze you how much you know and feel about a visit to the golden arches.

Top of Mind Questions

Tell your Martian visitor what they are going to experience at McDonald's. This is your chance to show off everything you know about all three dimensions of the experience. Once you have listed all the obvious things, pause, take a deep breath, and keep on going because there is a lot more to reveal.

Subconscious Probes

Now, it's time to find out what your inner mind has actually recorded down at the feeling level. Answer these questions and then add more of your own. What does the advertising message look like? What is the promise it implies? What do you hear when you are at the counter? What is on the wall to your left? What colour is the floor? How are the washrooms designed? What do the staff look like? How many are there and what do they say? And so on and so forth. Your Martian guest, with some well-posed questions, will find out that your subconscious had registered almost everything there was to know about McDonald's. And, you thought you only stopped off for hamburgers and fries.

Learning Applications

Do this exercise often. Do it on your way to the store or the bank. Raise your expectations up and look at them through the 3-D perspective. And, the next time you are engaged in customer research, wait for the pause that signals that the top of mind impressions are done, and then keep on going, deeper and deeper, to find out what your customers are recording about your business. And don't stop there, find out how those recorded messages are making them feel.

EXERCISE #2 TRUST: MONARCH OR BUTTERFLY?

When you are a Monarch, how do you act?

The Set-up

We are going to ask you to identify a place to which you are "loyal." Now, think about how you actually behave with this service provider. What do you do that would lead them to think you are truly loyal and should be added to their list of Monarchs?

Top of Mind Questions

What is it that I expect them to deliver and do they deliver it consistently? Do I really behave like a Monarch? Do I actually "pay" extra in time or money? Am I willing to forego the thrill of the new for the certainty of the old? When is the last time I gave this company the benefit of my market research? What would a competitor have to do to get me to transfer my loyalty?

Subconscious Probes

If you aren't really a Monarch, but just a repeat Butterfly at rest, ask yourself: Why? Are they just convenient and familiar, or do they meet some other motive well enough to cause me to be a repeat customer rather than a trusting, loyal one?

If, on the other hand, you really are a Monarch to this establishment, ask yourself: What is it they do to earn this level of trust and loyalty from you and how could they take further advantage of your interest in their success?

Learning Applications

Now go and listen to your customers and employees and experience their response to the same questions about doing business with or working with you. Customers think highly of companies where they are involved as an active player. Remember, the Monarch gives freely of their information and opinions related to your business. It takes time and effort, but the upfront investment pays off when you instinctively begin to think in 3-D as a matter of course.

EXERCISE #3 STRATEGY: THE CRYSTAL BALL

How are you feeling today and when did you first begin to feel this way? By the time a new behaviour starts to emerge, the feelings that influenced it have been well established.

The Set-up

Take recent copies of a selection of magazines (business, consumer, homemaker, specialty) and scan the headline stories and significant ads of every section looking for clues about customer response to service and how important service is.

Top of Mind Questions

After finishing with the magazines, ask yourself what possible effect could what you just read have on customer expectations for service providers, either full-service, service-when-I-ask, or self-service. Are these stories raising the level of expectation for more and more service? Are there elements of the stories that could be affecting the trust levels of the customers when it comes to service?

Subconscious Probes

Now, project into the future. What will the service culture of the future look like? What effect will today's influences have on the service sector? Will it increase the push for better, bigger, greater, feats of impossible service? And what will employees have to do in the future? Look into your crystal ball and try to predict what the expectations of your customers will look like in a couple of years.

Learning Applications

Service has already taken many of us to a place we can't afford. But, like everything, once it reaches its zenith, the pendulum will begin it's reverse swing. In fact, we think the move to more and more self-service is evidence that this reversal of the "super service" trend is already taking place. Where are you on this pendulum and what can you do to anticipate customer feelings? And, how ready are you for the emergence of the next trend those feelings may generate?

EXERCISE #4 THE SERVICE KALEIDOSCOPE: SNAPSHOTS IN 3-D

Never leave home without it—your service kaleidoscope, that is. Every time you see a great ad, super site, or are served by a fabulous person, twirl the three dimensions, and see how they focus and align.

The Set-up

Wonderful examples of each piece of the three dimensions are all around. The problem is in deciding how to adapt and apply them to your business. Every time you see something you are tempted to insert into your business mix, take a note, and then ask some probing questions before you act.

Top of Mind Questions

Does the element work as well when I imagine the three dimensions of the business? For instance, one store we love, called Hiker's Haven, has a great billboard on the side of its building. Every day, thousands of commuters, stuck in traffic, find themselves dreaming of a weekend walk as they inch past the billboard. The image is reinforced inside the store where membership applications for local walking groups are featured alongside the latest in walking and trail equipment. And the staff use their own products, and have the knowledge about what to buy and where to use it.

Subconscious Probes

How would the great idea which attracted me in the first place, translate to different settings? For instance, if Hiker's Haven were located in the downtown core, would the billboard be as effective? What would happen if this were a boutique in a department store? How would that affect expectations and delivery? What would happen if a new employee wasn't a hiker? Could they be trained at a reasonable cost?

Learning Applications

No idea is a great idea in isolation. Trust is built when the notion is seamlessly integrated in the three-dimensional experience. Before even thinking about implementing a new idea in your own business, imagine the process required to make it work in its original setting. Then, and only then, extend the concept to your three dimensions.

EXERCISE #5 A 3-D COMPANY: EMPOWERED OR ENTRAPPED?

There are many companies still operating as though the old models were still working, and treating things such as staff issues, in isolation. Are customer's comments becoming more negative? *Install a customer service program.* Is employee turnover up? *Get busy talking to employees.* Are expenses up and sales diminishing? *"Off with their heads!"* Each activity is taking place in isolation.

We've talked a lot about being a customer, and thinking like a shareholder may already be a reflex action. Here's something we bet you haven't done in a very long time, and you may find it a very humbling exercise indeed.

The Set-up

Go into the front lines of your own business and during a period of high customer traffic, take a shift and do a job that has direct customer contact. You must do this job with exactly the same training and tools as your staff received before they speak to their very first customer. Complete an entire shift dealing with whatever is thrown at you with whatever you have been given in the way of training and resources.

Top of Mind Questions

Would a new employee in this position have sufficient preparation to meet (or exceed) the expectations of the customers? What could I have done better for the other employees, customers, and shareholders if I had been more prepared? Were there things that I handled simply because of my age, position, maturity, and experience which might have been impossible for most others hired for this position?

Subconscious Probes

Are the wages, training, and working environment attracting the kind of employee I want to entrust my business to? What message am I really sending to customers with my current practices?

Learning Applications

If I described the newest front-line person to my shareholders would they be comforted knowing we have entrusted our assets to this person? How much customer goodwill could such an employee lose during their early learning curve? Consider the incremental gains that could be realized from better selected, trained, and yes, better paid, front-line staff.

ADAPT, BORROW, INTEGRATE, REJECT

Are these exercises all that are needed to keep your business in harmony? Are they everything you should do? Absolutely not. We hope you have found this book filled with ideas and suggestions, but before you set this book down and run out the door to "do" anything, let us tell you an instructional story about one client, who shall remain nameless.

Several times, during the 3-D presentation, this client interrupted the proceedings to murmur into his trusty Dictaphone. *"Tell Anne to do this." "Stop doing that." "Get a copy of the other training program." "Change the copy in Wednesday's ad."* At the conclusion of the session, we asked him to replay the recording and sum up what the learnings were. Fortunately, he discovered for himself that "doing" his itemized list would only exacerbate the disharmony already being felt by customers, lived by staff, and affecting shareholder profits.

Much of the failure of most change programs can be attributed to the fact that the company took someone else's process or tactics and tried to "shoehorn" them into their organization. What works for one corporation in their unique culture won't necessarily work in yours, even if you both offer similar products to what appears to be a similar customer. What works for your competitor with their customers may not work with yours.

By all means, take ideas and concepts from new programs, initiatives, and books like this one, but only after you have adapted them into your unique selling proposition, the harmony of your three dimensions, and the needs of your three stakeholders.

During the last few months of writing this book, we tried our concepts out on many unsuspecting (and some very suspicious) listeners. These discussions have only served to increase our understanding of how fast concepts are changing, how little we really understand about our customers, and how flexible we have to be in our approach to seeing the business.

Survival in the future will require courage. Courage to stick to what you believe to be best for your three stakeholders. Courage to insist that the three dimensions will always match. Courage to look beyond the short-term measurement of sales and profit and repeat business to the long-term foundation of trust.

CONCLUSION

THE NEXT TIME someone leaps over the service counter to impress the customer in front of you, will your inner voice applaud or groan?

When you count the number of customer names on your database will you hear the steady beat of the Monarch or the flutter of a million Butterfly wings?

When your next television or radio commercial brings tears to your eyes will it be because of the pull of the creative copy on your heartstrings or because you know how far the expectations being created in the mind of the customer are from the reality you can deliver?

Will you ever experience a renovated space, a greeter at the door, a piece of research, or a service excellence program in quite the same way again?

If this book has done what it was intended to do and what we promised at the beginning, the answer is a resounding no! Never again will you shop, plan your business, or look at any one of the three dimensions in quite the same way, not without "seeing" it where it matters most--in the inner, emotional self. That is the place where the Uh-oh feelings and disharmony create Butterfly behaviour, the place where all customers make the decision to trust and reward you with loyal Monarch behaviour, or fly away to try again another day, with someone new.

Tomorrow, like all too many other days in the past decade, customers will approach your door, influenced by the environment they live in. They are suspicious, wary, and ready to fly away at the first sign that you too, are not to be trusted. Because tomorrow, like all too many other days, the consumer in us all will find yet another news story about broken trust that will diminish ours. Perhaps it will be another sad tale of the luxurious private life of the televangelist living grandly off the contributions of fixed-income viewers. Or the public revelation that the president of the bank that proclaims, "We are changing," took home a huge increase in salary and benefits last year. Or a story about the "unfair practices" fine paid by a retailer whose sales consisted of first marking up the goods, before marking them down.

And so, tomorrow, you'll open your doors to a flock of Butterflies who are leery of your promises, more ready not to trust than to trust, and with a world of evidence that their behaviour is absolutely the safe way to act.

And yet, this same Butterfly is hoping that you will be the exception to the rule. That your business will be one to which they can return, confident that their expectations will be met and able to depend on your trustworthiness. Butterfly Customers want to, indeed, are yearning to trust. The tried and true pathways of the Monarch are attractive to a Butterfly weary of the consumer battlefield.

Trust is the commitment that binds customers to a business. It is the reason they return, or send others; care enough to offer criticism, advice, and free market research; are willing to pay extra in dollars, time, and energy. Without trust, there are no loyal Monarchs. Without loyal Monarchs there are only transient Butterfly Customers. With only Butterfly Customers your business is always at risk from one of the "ers"—Newer, Bigger, Better, Cheaper.

Will you be one of the stalwart few promising only that which you can deliver? Who avoid at all costs the use of Butterfly nets and untrustworthy practices? Who design all aspects of the business in anticipation of the subconscious reaction from customers and staff? Will you be a company that earns true loyalty from a Monarch Customer?

To do so is a worthy undertaking because loyal customers give you elasticity in your delivery. They allow you to make a mistake from time to time. They behave like partners instead of adversaries and they ultimately bring more customers to you. They are the low maintenance, high profit Monarchs on which any business can build a strong foundation.

To be trustworthy is the greatest gift you can give to a population of Butterfly Customers who are tired of the endless chase and are waiting to be metamorphosed into valued and valuable Monarchs. It is up to you. Do it and good luck.

THE FOLLOWING ARE some of the best books we have read and referred to in writing *The Butterfly Customer*. To help you select the ones which will provide you with the most valuable information and insights for your situation, we have provided our own idiosyncratic organization and commentary.

TRUST

When the "trust" word began popping up in our focus groups and on customer surveys, we searched the literature to learn what others had written about how customer's trust levels affect buying behaviour. Considering we are just emerging from two of the most customer-focused decades in history, there was remarkably little to be found. But some of what we did find was very good indeed. One of our favourite quotes from this assortment of titles is:

> "Trust is not an abstract, theoretical, idealistic goal forever beyond our reach. Trust—or lack of it—is inherent in every action that we take and affects everything that we do. Trust is

the cement that binds relationships...Without trust no compa-
ny can ever hope for excellence." [1]

There is still a great deal to be said about trust and we believe
there will be more research into the entire issue. Here are some
key titles available at the time of publication.

Fairholm, Gilbert W. *Leadership and the Culture of Trust.* Praeger, 1994.

Kouzes, James M. and Barry Z. Posner. *Credibility: How Leaders Gain and
Lose It, Why People Demand It.* San Francisco: Jossey-Bass, 1993.

Sonnenberg, Frank K. *Managing With A Conscience: How To Improve Performance Through Integrity, Trust, and Commitment.* New York: McGraw-
Hill, 1994.

BUSINESS INSIGHTS

It is hard to focus on trust when the fundamentals are being missed.
There are a plethora of books that speak to creating the kind of
atmosphere we find in a 3-D company. In our view, the guru remains
Peter Drucker, who was not only the first, but remains the best. This
quote sums up how we align with his views.

> *"Neither our concepts nor our tools are adequate for the con-
> trol of operations, or for managerial control. We need new
> measurements—call them a 'business audit'—to give us
> effective business control."* [2]

Our 3-D Audit owes its effectiveness to the words of wisdom
and processes of Drucker and to some of the other masters who
wrote these books.

---

[1] Frank K. Sonnenberg, *Managing With a Conscience: How to Improve Performance
Through Integrity, Trust, and Commitment* (New York: McGraw-Hill, 1993), pp.187-188.

[2] Peter Drucker, *Wall Street Journal Europe*, April 14, 1993.

Barrett, Derm. *The TQM Paradigm*. Denver: Productivity Press, 1995.

Drucker, Peter Ferdinand. *Managing in Turbulent Times*. New York: Harper & Row, 1980.

Drucker, Peter Ferdinand. *Post-Capitalist Society*. New York: HarperBusiness, 1993.

Kantor, Rosabeth Moss. *When Elephants Learn to Dance*. New York: Simon & Schuster, 1989.

Ogden, Frank. *The Last Book You'll Ever Read, and Other Lessons From the Future*. Toronto: Macfarlane Walter & Ross, 1993.

Peters, Thomas J. and Nancy Austin. *A Passion for Excellence: The Leadership Difference*. New York: Random House, 1985.

Peters, Thomas J. and Robert Waterman. *In Search of Excellence: Lessons from America's Best-Run Companies*. New York: Harper & Rowe, 1982.

Rifkin, Jeremy. *The End Of Work: The Decline of the Global Labor Force and the Dawn of the Post-Market Era*. New York: G.P. Putnam's Sons, 1995.

Treacy, Michael and Fred D. Wiersema. *The Discipline of Market Leaders: Choose Your Customers, Narrow Your Focus, Dominate Your Market*. Reading, Mass.: Addison-Wesley, 1995.

Zalwznik, Abraham and Manfred F.R. Kets de Vries. *Power and the Corporate Mind*. Chicago: Bonus Books, 1985.

KNOW THY CUSTOMER

While we may disagree with the call to action of some of the service books, there is no question that they have tremendous value in contributing to an understanding of the customer. These words of wisdom still ring true.

> *"Sure, one tenth of one percent of customers truly are evil and get their jollies or impress their friends by ripping off businesses. But if companies concentrate on protecting themselves*

from a small, unsavoury part of the population, what messages are they sending to the greater customer population?" [3]

Here are some of the books we have read and enjoyed. Our only caveat is, stop, take a deep breath before rushing to apply any specific actions to your situation.

Albrecht, Karl. *The Northbound Train: Finding the Purpose, Setting the Direction, Shaping the Destiny of Your Organization.* New York: AMACOM, 1994.

Bell, Chip R. and Ron Zemke. *Managing Knock Your Socks Off Service.* New York: AMACOM, 1992.

Bell, Chip R. *Customers as Partners: Building Relationships That Last.* San Francisco: Berrett-Koehler, 1994.

Berry, Leonard L. *Leonard L. Berry, on Great Service.* New York: Free Press, 1995.

Blanchard, Kenneth H. and Sheldon Bowles. *Raving Fans: A Revolutionary Approach to Customer Service.* New York: Morrow, 1993.

Brown, Stanley A. *What Customers Value Most: How to Achieve Business Transformation by Focusing on Processes That Touch Your Customers.* Toronto: John Wiley & Sons, 1995.

Davidow, William H. and Bro. Uttal. *Total Customer Service: The Ultimate Weapon.* New York: Harper & Row, 1989.

Foot, David K. *Boom, Bust and Echo: How to Profit from the Coming Demographic Shift.* Toronto: Macfarlane Walter & Ross, 1996.

Moseley, Lloyd W. *Customer Service: The Road to Greater Profits.* New York: Chain Store Age Books, 1972.

Popcorn, Faith. *The Popcorn Report: Faith Popcorn on the Future of Your Company, Your World, Your Life.* New York: Doubleday, 1991.

Popcorn, Faith and Lys Marigold. *Clicking: Sixteen Trends to Future Fit Your Life, Your Work, and Your Business.* New York: Harper Collins, 1996.

---

[3] Chip R. Bell, *Customers as Partners: Building Relationships That Last* (San Francisco: Berrett-Koehler, 1994).

Schilit, W. Keith. *Rising Stars and Fast Fades*. New York: Lexington Books, 1994.

Whiteley, Richard C. *The Customer-Driven Company: Moving From Talk To Action*. Reading, Mass.: Addison Wesley, 1991.

LEADERSHIP

It is encouraging to see how many of the well-received leadership books of the past few years have focused on how to be honest and forthright with employees. Another key theme is that the measurement of the leader is in the development of the employees, an important thought indeed for any organization which serves customers. Max De Pree, the leader of one of the most culturally developed companies in America put it this way.

> *"The measure of leadership is not the quality of the head, but the tone of the body. The signs of outstanding leadership appear primarily among the followers. Are the followers reaching their potential? Are they learning? Serving? Do they achieve the required results? Do they change with grace?"* [4]

Here are other leaders with messages worth exploring.

De Pree, Max, *Leadership Is an Art*. New York: Doubleday, 1989.

Heil, Gary, Tom Parker, and Rick Tate. *Leadership and the Customer Revolution*. New York: Van Nostrand Reinhold, 1995.

Kouzes, James M. and Barry Z. Posner. *The Leadership Challenge: How To Get Extraordinary Things Done in Organizations*. San Francisco: Jossey-Bass, 1987.

McCall, Morgan W., Michael Lombardo, and Ann Morrison. *The Lessons of Experience*. New York: Lexington Books, 1988.

Melohn, Tom. *The New Partnership*. omneo, Oliver Wright, 1994.

---

4 Max De Pree, *Leadership is an Art* (New York: Doubleday, 1989).

THE HISTORICAL PERSPECTIVE

The past has lessons, among them, that the world of customers and business may not be quite as rosy and uncomplicated as we would like to believe. Here are several tomes that put the present in a different light.

Benson, Susan Porter. *Counter Cultures, Saleswomen, Managers, and Customers in American Department Stores 1890-1940*. Chicago: University of Illinois Press, 1988.

Halberstam, David. *The Fifties*. New York: Villard Books, 1993.

Kanter, Donald L. and Philip H. Mirvis. *The Cynical Americans: Living and Working in an Age of Discontent and Disillusion*. San Francisco: Jossey-Bass, 1989.

Traub, Marvin and Tom Teicholz. *Like No Other Store: The Bloomingdale's Legend and the Revolution in American Marketing*. New York: Time Books, 1993.

Whirlpool Corporation. *The Whirlpool Report on Consumers in the '80s, America's Search For Quality*. 1983.

THE ULTIMATE BUSINESS BOOK

And when you really want to understand the confusing, paradoxical era of the Butterfly Customer, turn to the classics. No one yet has said it better than Lewis Carrol.

> *"It takes all the running you can do, to keep in the same place. If you want to get somewhere else, you must run at least twice as fast as that!"* [5]

---

[5] Lewis Carroll, *Alice's Adventures In Wonderland & Through the Looking Glass* (London: Grossett & Dunlap, 1946).

INDEX

Acceptance of loyalty invitation, 3, 4
Activities. *See also* Exercises
  behaviourial observation program, 140
  butterfly nets, 17
  competition, who are they, 125
  competitive challenge, response to, 128
  curiosity trait, 228
  decision making, 210
  economic atmosphere, 130
  faithfulness to unique selling proposition,
    115
  flexibility to staff, 117
  focus on the big picture, 110
  human resource system, 224
  leadership, 217
  management by walking around, 76
  media dimension
    campaign-strategy relationship, 147
    expectations-delivery relationship, 155
    tactics-goal relationship, 149
  Monarch customers, 40
  people dimension
    cost of insufficient staff, 196
    full service, 186
    involvement of front-line staff, 193
    make the impersonal, personal, 201
    service when asked for, 190
  physical dimension (crash test dummies),
    177
3D-audit
  allow auditors to get the facts, 89

feel employees' experience, 92
give staff permission to speak, 86
unique selling proposition, 108
Ad campaigns, 44, 45
Adapt ideas of others, 249, 250
Adjective checklists, 19, 20
American Express, 153, 154
Apple Computer, 147-149
Associations, 161-167
Automated teller machines (ATMs), 191
Automatic renewals, 15, 16

Baby boom, 134, 135
Bait and switch, 28, 29
Bank of Montreal, 71, 72
Banks, 163, 164
Barkow, Ben, 169
Basmaji, Joey, 220-222, 236, 237
Behaviourial observations, 138-140, 171
Ben & Jerry, 107
Berean Christian Bookstores, 81-100, 124
Bloomingdales, 112, 113
Blue Mountain Resorts, 235
Body Shop, 53-55, 57, 58
Book-of-the-month clubs, 16
Boom bulge, 134, 135
Boutique Jacob, 220-222, 236, 237
Branson, Richard, 55
Broken promises, 24, 27, 28
Buckley's, 133
Burden of constant vigilance, 42-44

Bush, George, 199
Butterfly customer, 1-10
Butterfly nets, 14-18

Cable & Wireless Communications, 110
Cable industry, 16
Carlton Cards, 139
Cashiers, 200, 201
Change merry-go-round, 172, 173
Changing environments, 173, 174
Changing prices, 174, 175
Chavez, Caesar, 7
Clinton, Bill, 199
Collective memory, 31, 32, 71, 72
Comfort zone, 197, 198
Company spokesmen, 53, 54
Competitive chaos, 123-128
Complaints, 8, 38
Consistent service priority, 195-197
Consumer focus groups, 7, 135-138
Consumer moods, 131-135
Consumer Report, 7
Corporate culture, 205. *See also* Internal
     affairs
Cost of mistrust, 42-44
Courage, 250
Cox, Carole, 77
Credibility, 46, 56
Credit card companies, 16
Cross-border shoppers, 182, 183
Culture. *See* Internal affairs
Curiosity, 227, 228
Customer comfort zone, 197, 198
Customer complaints, 8, 38
Customer profiles, 5
Cynical Americans, The, 24
Cynicism, 6, 7

Daniel Hechter, 61
Danier Leather, 113, 114
Decision making, 207-210
Deli counter, 196
Dell Computer, 109
Demographic models, 5
Develop your own program, 249, 250
Discipline of Market Lenders, The, 109
Discount programs, 174, 175
Disharmony, 60-62
Disney, 227
Display tactics, 162
Domain, 64, 65
Drucker, Peter, 104

Eaton's, 18, 107
Economic atmosphere, 128-130
Eddie Bauer, 190, 191
Emperor and His Clothes, The, 159
Employee empowerment, 220
Employees. *See also* Internal affairs, People
     dimension
  desirable traits, 227-229
  job descriptions, 224-226
  orientation, 232
  rewards and punishment, 234-236
  selection process, 226-229
  training, 229-234
  trust, and, 204
Entrepreneurs, 74
Exercises, 239-250. *See also* Activities
  design, 241
  front-line employee, 247-249
  service kaleidoscope, 247, 248
  strategy: crystal ball, 245, 246
  subconscious recorder, 242, 243
  trust: monarch vs. butterfly, 243, 244
Exit interviews, 171
Expectations contract, 78, 121-140
Exxon Valdez oil spill, 70

Faithful, 111-115
Fast, 117, 118
Feeling your business. *See* Exercises
Flexible, 115-117
Focus, 106-111
Focus groups, 7, 135-138
Foot, David, 134
Ford, Henry, 107
Four F behaviour, 106
Free with purchase bonus, 18
Full service, 184-188

Gap, The, 46
Gas station, 193
Gates, Bill, 199
George, Judy, 64, 65
Gifford, Kathie Lee, 41, 42
Golden Handcuffs, 14
Gregg, Alan, 128
Grocery stores, 172, 173

H_2O Plus, 54, 55, 59
Heirloom business, 134
Hidden expectations, 121-123
Honest Ed's, 62-64
Human instinct for trust, 41, 42
Human resources. *See* Employees

IKEA, 170, 173
Instant gratification mystery shop program, 235
Internal affairs, 205-218
  communications with staff, 211-215
  decision-making, 207-210
  leadership, 215-218
Internet, 9, 191

Job descriptions, 223-226
Job-shadowing, 92
Johnson and Johnson, 70
Joy of being of service, 228, 229

King Lear, 73
King, Rodney, 23
Kodak, 46

L'Oréal, 132
Leadership, 215-218
Leary, Timothy, 199
Leather Attic, The, 113
Lenscrafters Optical, 187
Low-trust mode, 31
Lying, 22, 23

MAC Cosmetics, 53-55, 58
Making do, 129, 130
Mama Toto, 58
Management by walking around, 77
Marcus, Stanley, 152
McDonald's, 107, 132, 141
Media dimension, 50, 51, 141-157
  campaign-strategy relationship, 145-147
  expectations-delivery relationship, 153-155
  involved/committed team, 150-153
  objective, 155, 156
  questions to ask yourself, 156, 157
  requirements of success, 145
  tactics-goal relationship, 147-150
Melnik, Cindy, 54
Microsoft, 176, 177
Miles, Dan, 82-87
Mirvish, Ed, 63
Mission statement, 216
Mistrust, 23
Moment of truth, 12
Monarch butterfly, 35-39
Mystery customers, 202, 203, 235

Nader, Ralph, 7
National Retail Federation, 131
Negative associations, 163-166
New Brunswick Tourism, 233

Nike, 109
Nordstroms, 46
Northern Reflections, 175, 176
Null, Jim, 81, 84, 87

Orientation, 232

People dimension, 52, 53, 181-204
  consistent service priority, 195-197
  customer comfort zone, 197, 198
  full service, 184-188
  make the impersonal, personal, 197-201
  mix and match service strategies, 194
  mystery customers, 202, 203
  self service, 191-194
  service to customer ratio, 189
  service when asked for, 188-191
Performance rewards, 234-236
Personal references, 8, 9
Personal trust quotient, 21
Peters, Tom, 11
Physical dimension, 51, 52, 157-179
  customer-friendly design, 168-176
  frustrations of change, 172-175
  real-world test, 176-178
  subconscious message (associations), 161-167
  traffic flow, 170
Popcorn, Faith, 7, 132
Popcorn Report, The, 8
Price changes, 174, 175
Princess Margaret Hospital, 168, 169

Rahola, 151
Real-time behaviours, 118
Record clubs, 16
Research techniques, 135-140
Reward and loyalty programs, 14, 15
"Reward me" motive, 132
Rewards and consequences, 234-236
Roddick, Anita, 53, 57, 58
Rotter, Julian, 31
Rubin, Warren, 74, 75
RuPaul, 53, 58, 59

Saturn, 133
Scepticism, 6, 7
Scratch & save coupons, 174
Search for Excellence, 11
Sears, 18, 127, 141
Second-hand stores, 130
Selection process, 226-229
Self service, 191
Selling behaviour, 106-110

Service-empowered people, 222
Service excellence myth, 11, 12
Service kaleidoscope, 49, 50
  feeling exercise, 247, 248
  media dimension, 50, 51. *See also* Media
    dimension
  people dimension, 52, 53. *See also* People
    dimension
  physical dimension, 51, 52. *See also*
    Physical dimension
Service Report, The, 37
Service station, 193
Service strategies
  full service, 184-188
  mix and match strategies, 194
  self service, 191-194
  service when asked for, 188-191
Service-when-I-ask-for-it model, 188-191
Shakespeare, William, 73
Shareholder equity, 13
Sign of the Dove, 37
Slogans, 107, 132, 141
Smith, Adam, 44
Staff. *See* Employees
Staff meetings, 215
Staff to customer ratio, 189
Stern, Howard, 199
Strategy, 103-120
Subconscious message, 161-167
Summit Corporation, 139

Tattered Cover, 39
Telephone companies, 166
Televangelist, 252
Tell the truth, 133
Thomson, Ken, 198
3-D audit, 81-101
  double-check the facts, 96
  feedback to staff, 96, 97
  feel customers' experience, 92
  feel employees' experience, 91, 92
  feel shareholder/owner's experience, 90, 91
  first activity, 216
  gauging the gaps, 94, 9
  get the facts, 87-89
  give staff permission to speak, 85
  increase comfort zone of team leaders, 84

  integrate perspectives of key stakeholders,
    94, 95
  involvement of owners/stockholders, 87
  locate source documents, 88
  multiple research methodology, 94
  objective, 82, 83
  overview, 77-79
  report to executive, 95-97
  steps, listed, 83
  timing, 83, 84
Three dimensions (3-D), 50
3M, 109, 110
Tips. *See* Activities
Tortoise and the hare, 105
Traffic flow, 170
Training, 229-234
Traub, Marvin, 112
Treacy, Michael, 109
Trust, 19-33, 204, 252
Trust account, 67-73
Trust quotient exercise, 21
Two-for-One, 7
Tylenol, 70

Uh-oh feeling, 25-27
Unique selling behaviour, 106-110
United Airlines, 141
Unreasonable service expectations, 25

Vending machines, 191
Vigilante consumer, 7, 8
Virgin Airlines, 55, 56

Wal-Mart, 41, 42, 69, 75, 76, 109
Walk the talk, 77, 216
Walton, Sam, 75, 76, 107, 198
Warehouse clubs, 29, 194
Warm fuzzies, 13
"Welcome to Retail", 233
Wiersema, Fred, 109
Wild Orchid, 68
Woolworth, F.W., 107
Word of mouth, 8, 9
Workbench, 74, 75
World Wide Web, 9

Zellers, 4